*From my
generation
to yours...
with love!*

From my generation to yours... with love!

GORDON B. HINCKLEY

Published by Deseret Book Company,
Salt Lake City, Utah 1974

ISBN No. 0-87747-512-1

Library of Congress No. 73-88637

Second Printing 1974

Lithographed by

DESERET PRESS

in the United States of America

Foreword

Often we are asked, "What is it like to grow up in the home of a General Authority?"

We would suspect that our home has not been unlike the homes of many other Latter-day Saints. Perhaps the only substantial difference has been that as our father has spoken throughout the Church we have seen him emulate the values and eternal principles of which he has spoken.

We can individually attest to the influence he has been in our lives and wish to share with other young people throughout the Church some of those truths, which can "kindle within each of us that divine spark which will give strength to our characters and fiber to our lives."

Kathleen H. Barnes
Richard G. Hinckley
Virginia H. Pearce
Clark B. Hinckley
Jane Hinckley

Walk in faith, and your example
will become another's strength.

Contents

Given in general conference, April 1970, and
subsequently reprinted, under the direction of the
First Presidency, for Churchwide distribution to youth

1

From My Generation to Yours . . .
With Love!

I should like to speak out across the land to the
youth who are the future of the Church and the hope
of the nations.

I found my theme in an airport in South America,
where we were delayed by late planes. I struck up a
conversation with a young man. His hair was long and
his face bearded, his glasses large and round. Sandals
were on his feet, and his clothing such as to give the
appearance of total indifference to any generally accepted standard of style.

I did not mind this. He was earnest and evidently
sincere. He was educated and thoughtful, a graduate
of a great North American university. Without employment, and sustained by his father, he was traveling through South America.

What was he after in life? I asked.

"Peace—and freedom," was his immediate response.

Did he use drugs?

Yes, they were one of his means to obtain the peace
and freedom he sought.

Discussion of drugs led to discussion of morals. He
talked matter of factly about the "new morality" that
gave so much more freedom than any previous generation had ever known.

He had learned in our opening introductions that I was a churchman; and he let me know, in something of a condescending way, that the morality of my generation was a joke. Then with earnestness he asked how I could honestly defend personal virtue and moral chastity. I shocked him a little when I declared that *his* freedom was a delusion, that *his* peace was a fraud, and that I would tell him why.

Our flights were called shortly after that and we had to separate. Since then I have thought much of our discussion. He is part of a challenging generation numbered in the millions who, in a search for freedom from moral restraint and peace from submerged conscience, have opened a floodgate of practices that enslave and debauch, and which, if left unchecked, will not only destroy individuals but also the nations of which they are a part.

I thought of this freedom and this peace when I recently faced a young man and a young woman across the desk of my office. He was handsome, tall, and manly. She was a beautiful girl, an excellent student, sensitive and perceptive.

The girl sobbed, and tears fell from the eyes of the young man. They were freshmen at a nearby university. They were to be married the next week, but not in the kind of wedding of which they had dreamed. They had planned that it would be three years from now, following graduation.

Now they found themselves in a situation both regretted and for which neither was prepared. Shattered were their dreams of schooling, the years of preparation they knew each needed for the competitive world that lay ahead. Rather, they would now have to establish a home, he to become the breadwinner at the best figure his meager skills could command.

The young man looked up through his tears. "We were sold short," he said.

"We've cheated one another," she responded. "We've cheated one another and the parents who love us—and we've cheated ourselves. We were betrayed. We fell for the rubbish that virtue is hypocrisy; and we've found that the new morality, the idea that sin is only in one's mind, is a booby trap that's destroyed us."

They spoke of a thousand thoughts that had crossed their minds in the fearful days and the anxious nights of the past few weeks. Should she seek an abortion? The temptation was there in the frightening contemplation of the ordeal that lay ahead. No, never, she had concluded. Life is sacred under any circumstance. How could she ever live with herself if she took measures to destroy the gift of life even under these conditions?

Perhaps she could go to some place where she was not known, and he could go on with his schooling. The child could be placed for adoption. There were excellent organizations that could assist in such a program, and there were good families anxious for children. But they had dismissed that thought. He would never leave her to face her trial alone. He was responsible, and he would meet that responsibility even though it blighted the future of which he had dreamed.

I admired his courage, his determination to make the best of an agonizing situation; but my heart ached as I watched them, bereft and sobbing. Here was tragedy. Here was heartbreak. Here was entrapment. Here was bondage.

They had been told of freedom, that evil was only a thing of the mind. But they found they had lost their freedom. Nor did they know peace. They had bartered their peace and their freedom—the freedom to marry when they chose to marry, the freedom to secure the education of which they had dreamed, and, more importantly, the peace of self-respect.

My young friend in the airport might have countered my story by saying that they were not smart. Had they been wise to the things available to them, they would not have found themselves in this sorry situation.

I would have replied that their situation is far from unique and that it is daily growing more acute. In 1968 there were 165,700 births to unwed schoolgirls in the United States alone, with an average annual increase of 12,000. (*Reader's Digest,* September 1970, p. 170.)

Can there be peace in the heart of any man, can there be freedom in the life of one who has left only misery as the bitter fruit of his indulgence?

Can anything be more false or dishonest than gratification of passion without acceptance of responsibility?

I have seen in Korea and Vietnam the tragic aftermath of war in the thousands of orphans, born of Korean and Vietnamese mothers and foreign soldier fathers. They have been abandoned, creatures of sorrow, unwanted, the flotsam of a miserable tide of immorality—tens of thousands, according to reports. Peace and freedom? There can be neither for him who has wantonly indulged nor for those left as the innocent and tragic victims of his lust.

Men are prone to gloat over their immoral conquests. What a cheap and sullied victory! There is no conquest in such. It is only self-deception and a miserable fraud. The only conquest that brings satisfaction is the conquest of self. It was said of old that "he that governeth himself is greater than he that taketh a city."

Are not the words of Tennyson still appropriate? "My strength is as the strength of ten, Because my heart is pure." ("Sir Galahad.")

You expect me to speak in this fashion. But listen to the conclusion of the renowned historians Will and Ariel Durant. Out of the vast experience of writing a thousand years of history, Dr. and Mrs. Durrant say:

> No one man, however brilliant or well informed, can come in one lifetime to such fullness of understanding as to safely judge and dismiss the customs or institutions of his society, for these are the wisdom of generations after centuries of experiment in the laboratory of history. A youth boiling with hormones will wonder why he should not give full freedom to his sexual desires; and if he is unchecked by custom, morals, or laws, he may ruin his life before he matures sufficiently to understand that sex is a river of fire that must be banked and cooled by a hundred restraints if it is not to consume in chaos both the individual and the group. (*The Lessons of History*, pp. 35-36.)

Self-discipline was never easy. I do not doubt that it is more difficult today. We live in a sex-saturated world. I am convinced that many of our youth and many older—but no less gullible—persons are victims of the persuasive elements with which they are surrounded: pornographic literature, which has become a $500 million a year business in this country alone, seductive movies that excite and give sanction to promiscuity, dress standards that invite familiarity, judicial decisions that destroy legal restraint, parents who often unwittingly push the children they love toward situations they later regret.

A wise writer has observed:

> A new religion is emerging throughout the world, a religion in which the body is the supreme object of worship to the exclusion of all other aspects of existence.
>
> The pursuit of its pleasures has grown into a cult . . . for its ritual no efforts are spared.
>
> We have bartered holiness for convenience, . . . wisdom for information, joy for pleasure, tradition for fashion. (Abraham Heschel, *The Insecurity of Freedom*, p. 200.)

Nakedness has become the hallmark of much public entertainment. It reaches beyond this into the realm of sadistic perversion. As one seasoned New York critic remarked, "It's not only the nudity; it's the crudity."

Can there be any reasonable doubt that in sowing the wind of pornography, we are reaping the whirlwind of decay?

We need to read more history. Nations and civilizations have flowered, then died, poisoned by their own moral sickness. As one commentator has remarked, Rome perished when the Goths poured over its walls. But it was "not that the walls were low. It was that Rome itself was low." (Jenkin Lloyd Jones.)

No nation, no civilization can long endure without strength in the homes of its people. That strength derives from the integrity of those who establish those homes.

No family can have peace, no home can be free from storms of adversity unless that family and that home are built on foundations of morality, fidelity, and mutual respect. There cannot be peace where there is not trust; there cannot be freedom where there is not loyalty. The warm sunlight of love will not rise out of a swamp of immorality.

As with the bud, so with the blossom. Youth is the seedtime for the future flowering of family life. To hope for peace and love and gladness out of promiscuity is to hope for that which will never come. To wish for freedom out of immorality is to wish for something that cannot be. Said the Savior, "Whosoever committeth sin is the servant of sin." (John 8:34.)

Is there a valid case for virtue? It is the only way to freedom from regret. The peace of conscience which flows therefrom is the only peace that is not counterfeit.

And beyond all of this is the unfailing promise of God to those who walk in virtue. Declared Jesus of Nazareth, speaking on the mountain, "Blessed are the pure in heart: for they shall see God." (Matthew 5:8.) That is a covenant made by him who has the power to fulfill.

And again, the voice of modern revelation speaks a promise—an unmatched promise that follows a simple commandment: ". . . let virtue garnish thy thoughts unceasingly." And here is the promise: "then shall thy confidence wax strong in the presence of God. . . .

"The Holy Ghost shall be thy constant companion, . . . and thy dominion shall be an everlasting dominion, and without compulsory means it shall flow unto thee forever and ever." (D&C 121:45-46.)

Just a word or two concerning this marvelous promise:

It has been my privilege on various occasions to converse with Presidents of the United States and other important men in other governments. At the close of each such occasion I have reflected on the re-warding experience of standing with confidence in the presence of an acknowledged leader. And then I have thought, what a wonderful thing, what a marvelous thing it would be, to stand with confidence—unafraid and unashamed and unembarrassed—in the presence of God. This is the promise held out to every virtuous man and woman.

I know of no greater promise made by God to man than this promise made to those who let virtue garnish their thoughts unceasingly.

Someone once remarked: "A world in which everyone believed in the purity of women and the nobility of men, and acted accordingly, would be a very different world, but a grand place to live in." (Channing Pollock.)

I assure you that it would be a world of freedom in which the spirit of man might grow to undreamed-of glory, a world of peace, the peace of clear con-science, of unsullied love, of fidelity, of unfailing trust and loyalty.

This may appear an unattainable dream for the world. But for each of you it can be a reality, and the

7

world will become so much the richer and the stronger for the virtue of your individual lives.

God bless you to realize this freedom, to know this peace, to gain this blessing. I promise you, as a servant of the Lord, that if you will sow in virtue, you will reap in gladness now and in all the years yet to come.

*A challenge given the
student body of Brigham
Young University*

2

How Lucky Can You Be!

In talking with a young man who is attending college, I said, "How are you getting along?" With a great smile on his face he said, "I'm getting along wonderfully! I have a good place to live—nothing fancy, but decent, comfortable, and fairly cheap. I'm taking the classes I want from teachers who know their stuff. And I have my eye on a wonderful girl." And then with consummate satisfaction he said, "How lucky can you be!"

How lucky can you be? In that question, which I suppose an English teacher might classify as slang, I find the text of some of the things I would like to say to youth.

Recently I was on a plane that traveled 600 miles an hour between New York and Salt Lake City. We left Kennedy Airport at six in the evening, rose faster than any bird could ever fly to an elevation of 35,000 feet, passed over the great cities of the East, and landed in Chicago an hour and forty-five minutes later. After a brief pause, we headed west again, out into the blackness of the night, across the Mississippi lowlands, and then over the vast prairies, relentlessly driven by the great jet engines, flying at 39,000 feet to take advantage of a tail wind that carried us to Salt Lake City in less than two and a half hours from take-

9

off to touch-down. The air was smooth, the seats were comfortable, the food was delicious.

Many of you have had similar experiences. This kind of everyday miracle has become commonplace to us. Like so many other marvelous things, we take it for granted.

We passed over Des Moines, skirted Omaha, and flew high over the rivers beside which a century ago our forefathers drove their oxen, traveling fifteen miles a day.

In my mind's eye I saw below the long wagon trains, dust rising with each turn of the huge wooden-spoked wheels. I saw the wagons circled in the evening, the oxen turned out to feed and water, the burdensome preparation of coarse food eaten with thanksgiving, the nursing of the sick, the burial of the dead among those who were leaving persecution to lay the foundation for all that we enjoy.

In imagination I saw my own grandfather—a young man who had been orphaned by a plague of smallpox of the kind that periodically swept the land in a day when there was no vaccine, no medicine, no hope— only fever, fear, death, and loneliness. With his brother and grandparents he had left Michigan, had gone to Springfield, Illinois, and then on to Nauvoo. There as a boy he met Joseph Smith, the man who changed his life and the lives of all the generations to follow him.

He witnessed in Nauvoo the resurgence of the old, ugly hatred, culminating in the murder of the Prophet. He saw Nauvoo threatened, then attacked, burned, and emptied of those who owned it.

He, with his young bride, started across Iowa, then followed the long trail up the Elkhorn and the North Platte in the direction of Fort Laramie. His wife grew pale and sick and died. With his own hands he chopped a tree beside the trail, made a coffin, dug a grave, left his sweetheart in a place he never again visited, and carried a three-month-old baby to the Salt Lake Valley.

I thought of him that night on the plane as we flew smoothly more than seven miles a minute over Nebraska and Wyoming I turned to Joshua, chapter 24, and read these words of the Lord given to an ungrateful Israel:

And I have given you a land for which ye did not labour, and cities which ye built not, and ye dwell in them; of the vineyards and oliveyards which ye planted not do ye eat. (Joshua 24:13.)

I thought of how appropriately that might be applied to our own generation. You and I live in a marvelous land for which we have not labored, and we dwell in cities which we built not, and eat of vineyards which we have not planted. How thankful we ought to be for the magnificent blessings we enjoy! Our society is afflicted with a spirit of thoughtless arrogance unbecoming those who have been blessed so generously.

If I have any desire in my heart, it is a desire to build in the lives and hearts of the young people of the Church a spirit of gratitude. Gratitude is a divine principle. The Lord has declared through revelation:

Thou shalt thank the Lord thy God in all things.

And in nothing doth man offend God, or against none is his wrath kindled, save those who confess not his hand in all things. . . . (D&C 59:7, 21.)

Absence of gratitude is the mark of the narrow, uneducated mind, It bespeaks lack of knowledge and the ignorance of self-sufficiency. It expresses itself in ugly egotism and frequently in malicious conduct.

In recent years we have witnessed the senseless destruction of millions of dollars of property by mobs of resentful, unthankful people whose only evident aim was to destroy the fruits of other men's labors. We

11

read accounts of people littering beaches and spoiling public playgrounds. We have seen thousands of acres of magnificent forests burned by the carelessness of smokers whose only evident concern has been the selfish pleasure gained from a cigarette.

Where there is appreciation, there is courtesy, there is concern for the rights and property of others. Without it, there is arrogance and evil. Where there is gratitude, there is humility as opposed to pride; there is generosity as opposed to selfishness.

How thankful we ought to be for the land in which we live!

While riding in that plane, I watched the moon. As it hung in the southern sky, it seemed almost within reach. Then I thought, this is the same moon that hangs over Asia, where there is hunger and oppression. I have seen the lean, frightened faces of refugees who, by some miracle, were able to get into Hong Kong. I have seen the children described by an English newspaper as children "whose eyes stare as if blind, whose legs and arms are like sticks of licorice, who neither cry nor laugh, and who weigh ten pounds at the age of ten years."

I saw that night the same moon that shines over India, where the per capita income per year is only about seventy dollars and where hunger stalks the land and men die young.

I saw the same moon that shines over Korea, where hangs the ever-present threat of war, where poverty is the rule rather than the exception, where the cold Siberian wind sweeps with misery and suffering.

I was returning on that plane from a conference in New Jersey, where we had met in comfort, and I thought of a conference we had held a year before in Seoul, Korea, where during all the hours of meeting the temperature in the hall never rose above 28 degrees.

How magnificently we are blessed! How thankful we ought to be! A bulletin of the Royal Bank of Canada said, in an article dealing with hunger in the world:

It is difficult for North Americans to understand the plight of people in underdeveloped countries, because we have never been desperately hungry. No one dies here of starvation. Elsewhere more than 1,500 million people go to bed hungry every night. . . . The fact is that not more than one in a hundred of the people in underdeveloped countries will ever, in all his life, have what a North American family would consider a good, square meal.

Reflect on that—and then get on your knees and thank the Lord for his bounties.

And to those young men and women for whom education is so relatively available, let me quote further:

In the world today only about one person in eight between the ages of five and twenty receives some formal education. . . . About 750 million persons at or over school age cannot read or write.

I ask, How lucky can you be?

Cultivate the spirit of thanksgiving in your lives. Make it of the very nature of your lives. It will impart an added dimension to your character that will give depth and strength.

The Lord has said, "Blessed are the meek, for they shall inherit the earth." (Matthew 5:5.) I cannot escape the interpretation that meekness implies a spirit of gratitude as opposed to an attitude of self-sufficiency, an acknowledgment of a greater power beyond oneself who is the giver of every good gift, a recognition of God and an acceptance of his commandments. This is the beginning of wisdom.

"Now therefore fear the Lord, and serve him in sincerity and in truth. . . ." (Joshua 24:14.)

This is my plea to you: Walk in thanksgiving before God and with appreciation before your associates. Add to your spirit of thanksgiving a great spirit of service, that you might bring to others the marvelous blessings that you yourself enjoy. As you look forward to your lives, as you prepare for the future, think of serving those beyond yourselves. Reach out in service to others.

Charles Malik, former president of the General Assembly of the United Nations, said:

> In this fearful age it is not enough to be happy and prosperous and secure yourselves. It is not enough to tell others, "Look at us, how happy we are. Just copy our system, our know-how, and you will be happy yourselves." In this fearful age you must transcend your system. You must have a message to proclaim to others. You must mean something in terms of ideas and attitudes and fundamental outlook on life. This something must vibrate with relevance to all conditions of man.

In my judgment, the greatest need of the world is a generation of men and women of learning and influence who can and will stand up and go forth and, in sincerity and without equivocation, declare that God lives and that Jesus is the Christ and that all men are brothers, with an obligation to serve one another.

How lucky can you be! How thankful you ought to be to use your lives in the service of others, and in so doing serve your God, of whose reality I testify as I invoke his choice blessings upon you!

Spoken to tens of thousands
of young men assembled
in a general priesthood meeting
of the Church

3

The Switches in Your Life

Wilford Woodruff records that in 1833 all of the priesthood of the Church met with the Prophet Joseph in a room only fourteen feet square, about the size of your bedroom.

Tonight, gathered in this and in some 750 other halls are more than 180,000 upon whom has been conferred that same priesthood. I would assume that among them there must be twenty-five or thirty thousand young men and boys. If the Spirit will give me utterance, I should like to speak to them.

At the outset, I should like to say that I am convinced that we have never had a more dedicated or more capable generation of young men in the history of the Church. Some of you older brethren may dispute that, which brings to mind the story of the boy who came down to breakfast one morning and said, χ"Dad, I dreamed about you last night."

"About me? What did you dream?"

"I dreamed I was climbing a ladder to heaven and on the way up I had to write one of my sins on each step of the ladder."

"And where did I come into your dream?" the father asked.

Said the boy, "When I was going up, I met you coming down for more chalk."

In various times throughout history, the Lord has chosen boys and trained them for the accomplishment of his marvelous purposes—such boys as Samuel, David, Joseph who was sold into Egypt, Nephi, Mormon, and Joseph Smith.

I believe that God has likewise chosen each young man and woman today for something of consequence in his grand design, perhaps not in the category of those I have named. But he loves you and he has a work for each of you to do.

How great, then, is your responsibility so to live that the Spirit of the Lord may dwell in you and that the Holy Ghost may speak through you!

The wonderful thing is that this is not beyond your capacity. The course of your life is not determined by great, awesome decisions. Your direction is set by the little day-to-day choices which chart the track on which you run.

Many years ago I worked in the head office of one of our railroads. One day I received a telephone call from my counterpart in Newark, New Jersey, who said that a passenger train had arrived without its baggage car. The patrons were angry.

We discovered that the train had been properly made up in Oakland, California, and properly delivered to St. Louis, from which station it was to be carried to its destination on the east coast. But in the St. Louis yards, a thoughtless switchman had moved a piece of steel just three inches.

That piece of steel was a switch point, and the car that should have been in Newark, New Jersey, was in New Orleans, Louisiana, thirteen hundred miles away.

So it is with our lives—a cigarette smoked, a can of beer drunk at a party, a drug taken on a dare, a careless giving in to an impulse on a date. Each has thrown a switch in the life of a young person that has put him on a track that has carried him far away from what

16

might have been a great and foreordained calling. And as Nephi said, ". . . thus the devil cheateth their souls and leadeth them away carefully down to hell." (2 Nephi 28:21.)

Do you remember the movie *The Sound of Music,* with its final, beautiful song, "Edelweiss"? It speaks of the flower of the Alps—"small and white, clean and bright, bless my homeland forever."

I brought home from Switzerland a package of Edelweiss seed. The seeds are tiny, like small dry flecks of pepper. But on the face of the package is pictured what they might become—the mature plant, the flower that grows high in the Swiss and Austrian Alps, that weathers the storms that rage through those mountains, that blooms beneath the snow, that gives beauty to Alpine slopes and meadows. These tiny seeds have within them the potential for vigorous and beautiful life. They have become the symbol of a sturdy people—"small and white, clean and bright," blessing a great land forever.

So it is with youth. There lies within each one of you an incalculable potential for good. The small day-to-day decisions will determine the course of your lives.

Therefore, *be smart.* The Lord has blessed each of you with greater capacity than you realize. Your I.Q. may not be the highest in the world. So what? Our jails are filled with clever people who were anything but smart. I have concluded that the work of the world is not done by intellectual geniuses. It is done by men of ordinary capacity who use their abilities in an extraordinary manner. As a member of The Church of Jesus Christ of Latter-day Saints, you have the obligation to seek learning and to improve your skills.

It matters not whether you choose to be merchant, teacher, carpenter, plumber, mechanic, doctor, or to follow any other honorable vocation. The important

17

thing is that you qualify to be a useful worker in society. It is so easy and so tragic to become a drifter, a drop-out. It is so challenging and so satisfying to be a producer. In so doing, you will bless not only your own life and the lives of those you serve, but you will also bring honor to and respect for the Church, for your identity as a Mormon will be recognized, and the image of the Church will be improved by reason of the opinion others have of you as you serve them. You cannot afford ever to do cheap or shoddy work.

Be clean. "Be ye clean that bear the vessels of the Lord." (D&C 38:42.)

With President Harold B. Lee we recently stood in the Garden of Gethsemane in Jerusalem where in agony the Lord foresaw the terrible suffering he must endure, suffering so intense that it caused even the Son of God to bleed at every pore. There he was mocked and betrayed and delivered into the hands of wicked men.

My dear young friends, do we not mock him anew if as Aaronic Priesthood bearers we come to the sacrament table with unclean hands and impure hearts to administer the emblems of his sacrifice?

As deacons, teachers, and priests, you cannot afford to sit around telling and laughing at dirty stories, reading pornographic literature, watching pornographic movies, abusing yourselves sexually, or stooping to immoral behavior of any kind.

Be clean for your own peace of mind. I spoke the other day with a young man who wished to go on a mission. In previous months he had been immoral. He and the girl with whom he had been associated thought they had done a clever thing. But he had come to realize that he had taken from her something precious that could never be restored, and that he had lost something of his own for which there was no compensation. With tears running down his cheeks he made his own judgment that he was unworthy to go into the world to teach to others a standard of behavior he had been unable to live himself. He had neither peace nor gladness.

Be clean, for the sake of your posterity. Someday each of you will meet the person of your dreams. If you truly love that person you would rather cut off your right arm than hurt him or her. Never lose sight of the fact that you are the line through which will pass the qualities of your forebears to the posterity who will come after you. Pause and think. Will those qualities be diminished or enhanced because of your behavior? Be clean, and your strength will be as the strength of ten because your heart is pure.

Be obedient, my dear young friends. Be obedient to the calls that come to you. We recently met with missionaries in England and Europe, more than a thousand of them. They are a miracle to me, a constantly renewing miracle. Their tremendous capacity, their courage in meeting obstacles, their quiet and effective powers of persuasion—how impressive they are! How do they do it? someone asked me. That capacity has come slowly, through obedience to the calls of the Church.

There is no small or unimportant duty in the kingdom of God. And out of the fulfillment of each responsibility comes the strength to undertake something new and more demanding.

"So nigh is grandeur to our dust, So near is God to man, When Duty whispers low, *Thou must,* the youth replies, *I can.*" (Ralph Waldo Emerson.)

Finally, *be prayerful.* The Lord has promised, "Be thou humble, and the Lord thy God shall lead thee by the hand, and give thee answer to thy prayers." (D&C 112:10.)

President Wilford Woodruff once declared:

It does not make any difference whether a man is a priest or an apostle if he magnifies his calling. A priest holds the keys of the ministering of angels. Never in my life, as an apostle, as a seventy, or as an elder, have I had more of the protection of the Lord than while holding the office of a priest.

Is it not a marvelous thing to contemplate that the priesthood of Aaron, which our young men hold, carries with it the right to the ministering of angels!

More than sixty years ago, a small boy on an Idaho farm went with his father to the field. While the father worked through the day, the boy amused himself with one thing and another. Over the fence were some old farm buildings derelict and tumbled down. The boy with imagination saw in them castles to be entered. He climbed through the fence and approached the buildings to begin his exploration. As he drew near, a voice was heard to say, "Harold, don't go over there." He looked to see if his father was around. He was not. But the boy heeded the warning. He turned and ran. He never knew what danger might have been lurking there, nor did he question. Having listened and heard, he obeyed.

That boy—Harold B. Lee—presided over The Church of Jesus Christ of Latter-day Saints. Through the years he listened, and the Lord magnified and protected and guided him by the whisperings of his Holy Spirit.

ᕁ For a period of three weeks in 1972 we walked together, I as his junior companion, in the ministry of the Lord. I give you witness of the workings of the Spirit in this prophet of our day whom the Spirit nurtured and cultivated and listened to through years reaching back to boyhood.

ᕁ Be prayerful, my friends, and listen. You may never hear a voice. You likely will not. But in a manner that you cannot explain, you will be prompted and blessed. For the Lord has promised, "I will tell you in your . . .

heart, by the Holy Ghost, which shall come upon you. . . ." (D&C 8:2.)

 ✔ Be prayerful, and you will know that God hears and answers—not always as we might wish him to answer, but with the passing of the years, there will come a realization as certain as the sunrise that he has heard and responded.

 ✓ And so, watch the switches in your life, the small but important day-to-day decisions. Be smart, my dear young friends. Be clean. Be obedient. Be prayerful. To do so will require a measure of discipline, the exercise of which will bring strength and capacity for great and demanding tasks that lie ahead of you in building the kingdom of God and in filling places of useful service in the work of the world. Your lives will be satisfying and your joy will be eternal. I so promise you as a servant of the Lord, and invoke upon you that sweet peace which comes from him alone.

BYU students are counseled
on getting more out of life by
putting more into it

4

You Get More Than You Give

Some time ago I stood in the American military cemetery outside the city of Manila in the Philippines. This is an awesome place. Like Flanders field, the crosses stand row on row in perfect symmetry. Beneath the smooth, green sod lie the remains of more than 17,000 American dead. Reaching out from the small chapel, like encircling arms, are two colonnades, done in classic style. Inscribed on the walls of these colonnades are the names of another 35,000 who died in the battles of the Pacific but whose remains were never found. In the foyers of these colonnades are beautiful maps that picture the geography of places once in the headlines of the world—New Guinea, Guadalcanal, the Marianas, Corregidor, Bataan, Iwo Jima—humid, hot, miserable places that once reeked with the smell of death and trembled with war.

I stood looking at one of those maps, done in glistening tiles of blue and gold and white. Then I glanced out across the rolling lawns with the marble crosses. I walked a few steps along the colonnade, observing the names, row upon row upon row, thousands upon thousands. My eye paused on one, the name of a boy who grew up not far from my own home, a boy who played ball, went to school, had fun, and then went to war; a boy whose plane fell in flames into an unexplored jungle or the vast ocean, no one knows just where.

His mother had received a terse telegram, and the tears had coursed her cheeks by night and day as her hair turned gray, then white. I saw her and her son in the imagined ghosts of that sacred, solemn place, and I walked away subdued and shaken with the thoughts of him and the more than 50,000 others there remembered who consecrated their lives that we might live in peace.

These men paid the price for our liberty. We have pretty largely forgotten them. As I walked along, a word passed through my mind, a word that has become trite and hackneyed in our vocabulary and largely meaningless: *sacrifice.* I thought, as I walked through that cemetery, of an article I had read a short time before in *Harper's* magazine under the title "What They'll Die For in Houston." It was written by an English teacher at a Texas university who had put a questionnaire to all of her students over a period of five years. She had asked these questions:

1. Why are you attending this university?
2. Are you satisfied with your situation? If not, in what way would you like to change it?
3. Is there anything you would be willing to die for? If so, what is it?

In answer to the first question, the students replied that their objective was to make friends, to improve their social status, or to get a job paying more money.

In reply to the second, they stated that they wanted the security that would give a family, a home, and a car. They evidently were not interested in challenges —only security.

To the third question they replied that they could not think of anything worth dying for, nothing at all.

I do not believe that these young men and women,

when faced with a crisis, would act any differently from those who are remembered in the cemetery outside Manila. And yet in view of their answers, so uniformly given, one wonders about their sense of values.

A bulletin of a major university recently listed the salaries that were then being offered graduates of that institution. It was interesting and gratifying to note how large these salaries were and how generous were the fringe benefits that accompanied them. I do not disparage the desirability of these salaries. We all value them. But I fear that we are becoming engrossed with salary alone.

The element of sacrifice is going out of our lives. I do not speak of giving one's life, although I believe that there are things worth dying for. I speak of giving one's self and one's substance without thought of any reward or compensation.

Selfishness is the basis of our troubles—a vicious preoccupation with our own comforts, with the satisfaction of our own appetites, with worship of what Paul Tillich calls the "idol of security."

If we are to bring peace into our lives, into our homes, and into our nation, we must cultivate some of the discipline of sacrifice.

I read some time ago the statement of one of the great editorial writers of America who said that the curse of America and the curse that hangs over the world can be expressed in a simple question that is given in response to almost any proposal that you make these days. Ask a man to serve here or serve there, or to do this or do that, and what is his response? "What's in it for me?"

A person is great only insofar as he serves and only insofar as he gives to the improvement of relations among our Father's children. Greatness comes of service.

Without sacrifice there is no true worship of God.

I become increasingly convinced of that every day. "The Father gave his Son, and the Son gave his life," and we do not worship unless we give—give of our substance, give of our time, give of our strength, give of our talent, give of our faith, give of our testimonies.

In the Church we have a great missionary program. I think that if nothing else came of this than to take out of the lives of our young people the vicious selfishness that is so prone to afflict youth, all that we put into it would be worth it. What a marvelous thing it is to have a young man or woman go out into the world, at the time of life when he or she is most prone to think of self alone, and lose himself or herself in the service of others and in the service of God.

In a testimony meeting in Taipei, we sat in a cold room with a group of thirty or forty missionaries. One fine-looking young man from Hawaii, who came from a comfortable home where he had been spoiled and pampered, stood up before that group and made this statement, which has become a classic to me: "I thank the Lord for eyes to see, and mouth to speak, and feet to carry me from door to door, to teach the gospel of Jesus Christ to the wonderful people of China."

This is the spirit we need. You are great when you have that great spirit.

May God bless all of our young people with a spirit of serving. If it involves sacrifice, don't worry about it —it really isn't sacrifice. That is the marvelous thing. It isn't sacrifice, because when you give, you always gain more than you give. That young man was going without the comforts he knew at home, but there had come into his heart and soul a priceless compensation. It is not sacrifice when you gain more than you give, and that is exactly what he was doing.

What a tremendous thing it is to be a part of a church that has a great heritage, a tremendous background, that speaks of faith and courage and sacrifice and giving. If we ever lose it, we had better close up shop. Without sacrifice there is no true worship.

Selfishness is the cause of most of the domestic problems that afflict so many homes today.

I sat for hours one day listening to two people who had been divorced but who said they still loved one another. First I talked to the husband. He sobbed and sobbed for his wife and then talked about what a terrible woman she was. Then I talked to the wife. She cried over her husband and then talked of what a stingy man he was. After I had listened to them individually, I brought them together and said to them, "There is only one thing wrong with you. You're just too miserably selfish. You are unwilling to sacrifice for one another. You are unwilling to lay aside your own little comforts in order to accommodate one another."

I heard a wise man say on one occasion that the answer to marital problems is not divorce but repentance. Repentance in cases of this kind involves giving up something in the interest of one's companion.

The roots of evils in traffic today lie in selfishness. The man who cannot sacrifice five minutes in getting somewhere and who speeds on the highway without respect for the rights of others is the man who causes many of our problems. This is nothing but selfishness. It is nothing but an unwillingness to show respect for the interests of others.

Sacrifice, service, decency, goodness, helpfulness— these are the basis of friendship. One of the lines that has affected me most in all the literature that I have read is that great statement of Sidney Carton, in Dickens' *A Tale of Two Cities.* Carton is a man who walked to the guillotine in behalf of a friend and, when asked about it, said, "It is a far, far better thing that I do, than I have ever done; it is a far, far better rest that I go to, than I have ever known."

Most of us are not called on to give our lives for

others, but we are called on to serve, even at personal inconvenience, every day of our lives.

⋎ To youth, as you go forward with your ambitious programs, forget yourselves now and again. Lay aside your selfishness; lose yourself in the service of others and in some great cause. ". . . He that loseth his life for my sake shall find it." (Matthew 10:39.)

Well might we remember a great conclusion from Phillips Brooks: "How prudently most men creep into nameless graves, while now and again one or two forget themselves into immortality."

⋎ God bless you as you go forward with your lives, not only to improve your skills that you may command a price that will care for your needs, but, more importantly, that you will develop the spirit of giving of yourselves—of your substance, of your time, of your talents—without consideration of reward, for the blessing of our Father's children, wherever you may find them.

5

"With All Thy Getting . . ."

Recently I strolled about the campus of one of our great universities. I was impressed with the splendor of the buildings, the immaculate laboratories, the teaching theaters, the magnificent library, the dormitories, the gymnasiums. But I was more impressed with the students—handsome young men and beautiful young women, serious and intent and earnest.

These are a few of the hundreds of thousands who are attending college at this time. I am awed by the great forces of knowledge they represent. Never before have so many been educated in the learning of the world.

What a marvelous thing this is—the intensive schooling of a large percentage of the youth of the land, who meet daily at the feet of able instructors to garner knowledge from all the ages of man. The extent of that knowledge is staggering. It encompasses the stars of the universe, the geology of the earth, the history of nations, the culture of peoples, the languages they speak, the operation of governments, the laws of commerce, the behavior of the atom, the functions of the body, and the wonders of the mind.

With so much available knowledge, one would think that the world might well be near a state of perfection. And yet we are constantly made aware of the other side of the coin—of the sickness of our society, of the contentions and troubles that bring misery into the lives of millions.

Each day we are made increasingly aware of the fact that life is more than science and mathematics, more than history and literature. There is need for another education, without which the substance of our secular learning may lead only to our destruction. I refer to the education of the heart, of the conscience, of the character, of the spirit—these indefinable aspects of our personalities that determine so certainly what we are and what we do in our relationships one with another.

And so I would like to communicate with our young people, those in the Church and those out of the Church—with the youth of America and of other good lands.

Some forty years ago while living in England I belonged to the London Central YMCA. I suppose that old building has long since gone, but I can never forget the words that faced us in the foyer each time we entered. They were the words of Solomon: ". . . with all thy getting get understanding." (Proverbs 4:7.)

I commend them to you.

Understanding of what? Understanding of ourselves, of the purposes of life, of our relationship to God who is our Father, of the great divinely given principles that for centuries have provided the sinew of man's real progress!

I cannot discuss them all, but I would like to suggest three. I offer them not in a spirit of preachment but in a spirit of invitation. Let these be added to your vast store of secular knowledge to become cornerstones on which to establish lives that will be fruitful, productive, and happy.

The first I mention is *gratitude,* which we discuss elsewhere in this book.

Associated with gratitude is *virtue*. I think they are related because he who is disposed to shun virtue lacks appreciation of life, its purposes, and the happiness and the well-being of others.

One of our great national magazines once stated the following:

> We are witnessing the death of the old morality. The established moral guidelines have been yanked from our hands. . . . We are left floundering in a money-motivated, sex-obsessed, big-city dominated society. We must figure out for ourselves how to apply the traditional moral principles to the problems of our times. Many find this burden too heavy. (*Look,* September 1963, p. 74.)

Heavy though it be, there is a way to apply traditional moral principles in our day. For some unknown reason there is constantly appearing the false rationalization that at one time in the long-ago, virtue was easy and that now it is difficult. I would like to remind you that there has never been a time since the creation when the same forces were not at work that are at work today. The proposal by Potiphar's wife to Joseph in Egypt is not essentially different from that faced by many a young man and woman in our day.

The influences today may be more apparent and more seductive, but they are no more compelling. You cannot be shielded entirely from these influences. They are all about us. Our culture is saturated with them. But the same kind of self-discipline exercised by Joseph will yield the same beneficial result. Notwithstanding the so-called new morality, notwithstanding the much-discussed changes in our moral standard, there is no adequate substitute for virtue. The old standard is challenged on every campus in America as it is in Europe. But God has not abrogated his commandments.

The violation of these commandments in this, as in any other age brings only regret, sorrow, loss of self-respect, and in many cases tragedy. Rationalization and equivocation will not erase the cankering scar that blights the self-respect of a young man who takes that virtue which he can never replace. Self-justification will never mend the heart of a young woman who has drifted into moral tragedy.

In April 1942, the First Presidency of the Church issued a message that has the tone of scripture. I commend it to you:

To the youth of the Church. . . above all we plead with you to live clean, for the unclean life leads only to suffering, misery, and woe physically—and spiritually it is the path to destruction. How glorious and near to the angels is youth that is clean; this youth has joy unspeakable here and eternal happiness hereafter.

I thought of this as I observed these thousands of handsome young men and beautiful women on the university campus the other day. And I thought of a wise statement from the scripture: ". . . the commandment is a lamp; and the law is light. . . ." (Proverbs 6:23.)

You of marvelous promise, you young men and women of great ability, do not mock God. Do not flout his law. Let virtue be a cornerstone on which to build your lives.

I turn next to *faith*. I do not mean it in an abstract sense. I mean it as a living, vital force with recognition of God as our Father and Jesus Christ as our Savior. When we accept this basic premise, there will come an acceptance of their teachings and an obedience that will bring peace and joy in this life and exaltation in the life to come.

I do not regard this as a theological platitude. I regard it as a fact of life. It can become the very wellspring of purposeful living. Can you imagine a more compelling motivation to worthwhile endeavor than the knowledge that you are a child of God, the Creator of the universe, our all-wise Heavenly Father who expects you to do something with your life and who will give help when help is sought for?

These wonderful college years are years of learning. Jesus said: ". . . learn of me. . . . For my yoke is easy, and my burden is light." (Matthew 11:29-30.)

⚔ I should like to suggest that you follow that injunction given by the Son of God. With all of your learning, learn of him. With all of your study, seek knowledge of the Master. That knowledge will complement in a wonderful way the secular training you receive and give a fullness to your life and character that can come in no other way.

We were aboard a plane some years ago flying between Honolulu and Los Angeles. It was in the days when only propeller-driven aircraft were available. About midway in our journey one of the motors stopped. There was a decrease in speed, a lowering in altitude, and a certain amount of nervousness among those aboard. The simple fact of the matter was that much of the power was missing and the hazards were increased accordingly. Without that power we could not fly high, fast, nor safely.

It is so with our lives when we discount the need for faith and disregard knowledge of the Lord.

Passive acceptance is not enough. Vibrant testimony comes of anxious seeking. Strength comes of active service in the Master's cause. "Learn of me" was Jesus' injunction. He further declared that he that doeth the will of the Father "shall know of the doctrine, whether it be of God, or whether I speak of myself." (John 7:17.)

ﹶAnd so, while you read math and physics and chemistry, read also the Gospels of the New Testament. And read the testament of the New World, the Book of Mormon, which was brought forth by the power of God "to the convincing of the Jew and the gentile that Jesus is the Christ."

32

To every young man and woman I should like to say, take upon yourself the name of the Lord and then with faith go forth to teach with relevance that which will affect the lives of men and bring peace and joy to the world. The need of the world is a generation of men of learning and influence who can stand up and in sincerity and without equivocation declare that God lives and that Jesus is the Christ.

And so, my dear young friends, I suggest to you with all earnestness that as you pursue your secular studies you add another dimension to your life, the cultivation of the spirit. God bless you with that peace which comes from him alone, and that growth which comes of sharing with others that which is most precious, your faith.

*The response to
an assigned subject
to speak on at BYU*

6

Caesar, Circus, or Christ?

Brigham Young stated on one occasion that our people came willingly to these valleys because they had to. I feel a little that way about the subject of this discussion. The title given me was "Caesar, Circus, or Christ?" I was given a case from which to build a talk. It reads in part as follows:

Mark thought of Sunday night's sacrament meeting and the resolutions and promises he'd made to himself after being so inspired.

"How many times have I made promises to myself and broken them time after time?" he thought.

Boisterous, loud laughter suddenly made Mark aware of the "friends" he was with. The swells of laughter increased. Off-color jokes had been gaily passed back and forth. . . .

He reflected now on a similar experience last Friday. He and two friends were taking their girls to a movie. The choices available were poor. He had read enough of the advertisements and reviews to know they portrayed the slick and slimy. But again he held back, not revealing his real thoughts about wasting his time in a trashy movie.

"I'm not an angel, but I've got to stand for something. Why do I sit here and listen to this garbage?" He wanted to get up and walk out—to change the subject—to tell them all off. But he just sat there, not having the courage to do anything.

That is the case as it was presented to me. My first reaction on reading it was simply, "Are we mice or are

34

we men?" I wondered whether it was worthy of discussion before this large body. It appeared superficial. But the more I thought about it, the more serious it became as representative of the decisions each of us constantly face. It reminded me of the two college boys who were discussing what they should do tonight. One suggested they flip a coin—"Heads we go to the movie; tails we go to the dance. If it stands on edge, we study."

Seriously, there is involved in such simple decisions the entire question of what we do with our lives. It is not so much the major events as the small day-to-day decisions that map the course of our living.

And by what standards shall we make those decisions? By the standards of *Caesar,* meaning the standards of the state, as politicians have established those standards? By the standards of the *circus,* meaning the standards of the self-seeking masses? Or shall we make our decisions by the standards of *Christ,* the Son of God, who came in the meridian of time as the one true lawgiver?

What are the standards by which *you* will govern *your* life?

We hear much today of consensus. It simply means agreement, a meeting of the minds. The doctrine is abroad that whatever bears the brand of consensus is right and good. There never was a more serious fallacy. Fifty thousand Frenchmen can be wrong, as can fifty million Americans, or 350 million Chinese. I think it was Bertrand Russell who observed that "the curse of America is conformity."

Consensus in matters of public and private morality is largely fruitless and often detrimental unless its roots are anchored in eternal, God-given truth.

Specifically with reference to young people, particularly those who are attending college or busy establishing themselves in the business world, there is little spare time, but the use to which you put that spare time will in large measure determine the quality of your life and the contribution you make to the world of which you are a part.

And so I should like to suggest three standards by which to judge each of the decisions that determine the behavior patterns of your life. These standards are so simple as to appear elementary, but I believe their faithful observance will provide a set of moral imperatives by which to govern without argument or equivocation each of our actions and which will bring unmatched rewards. They are:

1. Does it enrich the mind?
2. Does it discipline and strengthen the body?
3. Does it nourish the spirit?

Now to the first, *Does it enrich the mind?* I was tremendously impressed a few years ago with President David O. McKay's closing remarks at general conference. He said, among other things:

> Wisdom comes through effort. All good things require effort. That which is worth having will cost part of your physical being, your intellectual power, and your soul power. "Ask, and it shall be given you; seek, and ye shall find; knock and it shall be opened unto you." (Matthew 7:7.) But you have to seek, you have to knock. On the other hand, sin thrusts itself upon you. It walks beside you, it tempts you, it entices, it allures. . . . Evil seeks you, and it requires effort and fortitude to combat it. But truth and wisdom are gained only by seeking, by prayer, and by effort. (*Conference Report,* October 1965.)

I once made an appeal to President McKay in behalf of a young man who was about to be excommunicated from the Church because of transgression. I ventured the opinion that the young man had been trapped in a moment of weakness. President McKay responded that the thought had been father to the act, and that which the young man had done had not occurred only in a moment of weakness, but over an extended period of thinking about it.

There is something tragic in the case study presented for this discussion; something terribly disappointing when two young men waste their precious money and their yet more precious time and that of their girl friends at a movie described as "slick and slimy." We have so much of that kind of entertainment because the consensus tolerates and even demands it.

It is so likewise with the things we read. I recently observed a group of young men poring over magazines and paperbacks at a drugstore newsstand. Judged by the titles and the art on the covers, these publications were at best worthless and at their worst pornographic. Who can doubt the corrosive effect of the reading of salacious literature and the watching of salacious pictures?

I would not have you find your relaxation only in reading the classics or the scriptures, though these deserve a wider reading and will bring an incomparable enrichment. But there is much else. Among our current periodicals there are still a few whose reading will enrich your minds and broaden your understanding; and among current book publications there may be found much that is interesting, provocative, and inspirational. These may require in their reading a greater measure of concentration, but they will also bring a greater reward.

I looked the other day with wonder and affection on a 1916 Model T Ford. It brought back a thousand memories of my childhood, for this was the first automobile we ever owned in our family. It was a thing of wonder when we were children. Young people today know little of these cars. They had no battery, and the source of electricity was a magneto. At night the intensity of the light depended on the speed of the motor. If the motor was kept running at high speed, the lights were bright. If the motor slowed down, the lights became a sickly yellow.

It is so with our minds. If we keep them sharpened on good literature and uplifting entertainment, development is inevitable. If we starve them with the drivel of miserable shows, cheap literature, and off-beat entertainment, they become poor indeed.

It was Ruskin who observed: "The greatest reward is not what we receive for our labor, but what we become by it."

I move now to my second standard of judgment: *Does it discipline and strengthen the body?*

At one time I worked for the railroad. My superintendent was an extremely capable man, a graduate in engineering from one of our great universities. He distinguished himself as chief engineer of that railroad and then moved on to become an officer of one of the two or three largest railroad systems in the nation. He was a man of tremendous ability and tremendous promise. But something went wrong. He began to drink. He thought he could be temperate and take a nip only now and again. His last days were spent on skid row in Chicago where he died in a flophouse, not many miles from the doors of that institution from which he had walked not many years earlier as a *cum laude* graduate. Can there be a greater tragedy in life than this?

It was said of old that "he that governeth himself is greater than he that taketh a city." Shakespeare noted that "there is a tide in the affairs of men, which, taken at the flood, leads on to fortune." There is likewise an ebb in the affairs of men which, ridden with the drifting wave, leads to destruction.

Two missionaries who were teaching an older couple were told by the man at the end of the lesson not to come back. Before leaving one of them turned and said, "May I ask just one question? Why?" To this the man replied, "I guess we love the jug more than we love God." At this the wife broke down and wept, saying, "Why can't we be good people, too?"

I am not suggesting that any of our youth are heading for the slough of alcoholism. But I am suggesting that no young man or woman can afford to make a decision that involves the drinking of beer or any alcoholic beverage or the taking into his or her body of any other substance that will fail to strengthen.

It becomes a shocking footnote on our society when more than 40 percent of the young men of America are disqualified for military service on the basis of physical, mental, or moral deficiencies. How we need to shape up and tighten our self-discipline!

Marvelous is the promise of the Lord that those who walk "in obedience to the commandments, shall receive health in their navel and marrow to their bones; And shall find wisdom and great treasures of knowledge, even hidden treasures; And shall run and not be weary, and shall walk and not faint." (D&C 89: 18-20.)

Let this, then, become a standard by which to make decisions regarding our actions: Does it discipline and strengthen the body?

I move now to my concluding standard: *Does it nourish the spirit?*

It was Elihu, Job's comforter, who declared, ". . . there is a spirit in man: and the inspiration of the Almighty giveth them understanding." (Job 32:8.)

How shall we determine that which will nourish the spirit? Moroni gives the answer:

For behold, the Spirit of Christ is given to every man, that he may know good from evil; wherefore, I show unto you the way to judge; for every thing which inviteth to do good, and to persuade to believe in Christ, is sent forth by the power and gift of Christ; wherefore ye may know with a perfect knowledge it is of God. (Moroni 7:16.)

Here is the kernel of the whole matter. We need not worry about consensus, or reason, or opinion in matters of right and wrong. "The Spirit of Christ is given to every man, that he may know good from evil." Most of us know better than we do. As we discipline ourselves in line with our knowledge, in line with the inner convictions of our hearts, rather than the inclination to follow the crowd, we grow.

A student asked me once whether I believe in evolution. I replied that I worry little about organic evolution, but I am very much concerned with the evolution of man, the child of God. And I quoted to him these marvelous words from revelation that I feel are of the very essence of this discussion:

> And that which doth not edify is not of God, and is darkness.
> That which is of God is light; and he that receiveth light, and continueth in God, receiveth more light; and that light groweth brighter and brighter until the perfect day. (D&C 50:23-24.)

This is the evolution that comes of decisions that nourish the spirit—decisions made according to the great everlasting standards which, regardless of the reasonings of moralists and philosophers, regardless of the consensus of those who establish public policy and mold public opinion, are eternal in their application and eternal in their benefits, for they come from the God of heaven, our Eternal Father, who has implanted in each of his children something of his divine nature.

Well might we consider the words of Polonius to his son:

> This above all: to thine own self be true,
> And it must follow, as the night the day,
> Thou canst not then be false to any man.

Or the words of Joshua, who, old in years and wise in experience, gathered together a new generation who were forgetful of the trials of the past while living in the luxury of the present. To them Joshua said, in the name of the Lord, ". . . choose you this day whom ye will serve; . . . but as for me and my house, we will serve the Lord." (Joshua 24:15.)

This, my brethren and sisters, is our divine right—to choose. This is our divine obligation—to choose the right. God give us the strength, the courage, the faith in all of our choices to choose that which will enrich the mind, strengthen and discipline the body, nourish the spirit, and thus give us growth and joy in this life and eternal life in the world to come.

*The first Area General Conference
of the Church was held in
Manchester, England, in 1971.
These comments were made to
a special session for women and girls.*

7

To Women of a Noble Birthright

I need not tell you that this is a very exciting experience. I was on a mission here thirty-eight years ago, and I have been looking at you and trying to gauge your ages, and wondering how many of you slammed doors in my face back in those days.

I would like, if the Lord will bless me, to talk about two or three things very quickly. I would like to say that in the home where there are children, there ought to be good reading, inspirational reading. I count it a great privilege and blessing in my life that I was reared in a home where there was much to be read—good magazines, many books. My father had a library in his home in which there were more than a thousand volumes of good literature. We were never compelled to read, but the very atmosphere with which we were surrounded inclined us in that direction.

As I came into the conference hall this morning, I said to a young man, "Why are you so happy today?"

He said, "I'm going to get married."

"Oh, is that so? When did you get engaged?"

He replied, "Last night."

"How long have you gone with that girl?"

"Oh, about two years, but last night she looked so

beautiful in a formal gown that I had the courage to ask her to marry me."

I have been on the continent of Europe for a month traveling in the missions in Germany and Austria, Switzerland and Italy. I have seen by the thousands shaggy, unkempt, sex-oriented, drug-using young people. Many of those traveling are not in those categories, but many are. We live in a sex-saturated world, and you don't have to travel far to see evidence of this.

I would like to say to our young women—you of the noble birthright, you who have been baptized for the remission of your sins, you who have entered into covenant with God as his daughters—keep yourselves unsullied from the world. That which is cheaply gained will be cheaply cast aside.

We have in the United States a newspaper columnist named Abigail van Buren. Her writings are published across the world. She is one of those who give advice to the troubled. A young lady wrote her and said that her boyfriend wanted her to prove her love, and this was Abby's response—plain-spoken, but good:

Girls need to prove their love through illicit sex relations like a moose needs a hat rack. Why not "prove your love" by sticking your head in the oven and turning on the gas or playing leapfrog in the traffic? It's about as safe.

Clear the cobwebs out of your head. Any fellow who asks you to "prove your love" is trying to take you for the biggest, most gullible fool who ever walked. That "proving" bit is one of the oldest and rottenest lines ever invented.

Does he love you? It doesn't sound like it. Someone who loves you wants whatever is best for you. But now figure it out. He wants you to: commit an immoral act, surrender your virtue, throw away your self-respect, risk the loss of your precious reputation, and risk getting into trouble.

Does that sound as though he wants the best for you? This is the laugh of the century. He wants what he thinks is best for him! He wants a thrill he can brag about at your expense. Love? Who's kidding whom?

43

A guy who loves a girl would sooner cut off his right arm than hurt her. In my opinion, this self-serving so-and-so has proved that he doesn't love you.

The predictable aftermath of "proof" of this kind always finds Don Juan tiring of his sport. That's when he drops you, picks up his line, and goes casting elsewhere for bigger and equally silly fish.

If he loves you, let him prove his love by marching you to the altar.

I think that is well said.

I have another statement of Abby's. I offer it because all who wish to be married may not have the opportunity. For these and others Abby has set forth some sound principles. Said she:

The key to being popular with both sexes is: Be kind. Be honest. Be tactful. If you can't be beautiful, . . . be well groomed, tastefully attired, thin of figure, and keep a smile on your face.

Be clean in body and mind. If you're not a brain, try harder. If you're not a great athlete, you can be a good sport. Try to be a standout in something. If you can't dance or sing, learn to play an instrument.

Think for yourself, but respect the rules. Be generous with kind words and affectionate gestures, but save the heavy artillery for later. You'll be glad you did. If you need help, ask God. If you don't need anything, thank God.

You young women of the noble birthright, you the hope of the Church, you the mothers and grandmothers and great-grandmothers of the sons and daughters of Israel who are yet to come, keep yourselves worthy of the blessings of God. Keep yourselves pure and virtuous and good and decent and sweet and wonderful; and as a servant of the Lord I do not hesitate to promise you that you will be loved and respected and honored. You will be grateful and get on your knees with tears in your eyes and thank your Father in heaven for his watchful care over you and for the marvelous blessings which will be yours.

Reference is made these days to "women's lib." I

believe in the liberation of women. I think the greatest statement ever made on the liberation of women was made by the Prophet Joseph Smith when he declared to the women of the Church these marvelous words: "I now turn the key in your behalf in the name of the Lord, and this society [the Women's Relief Society] shall rejoice, and knowledge and intelligence shall flow down upon women from this time henceforth."

My dear sisters, out of the restored gospel of Jesus Christ has come a liberation of women that is marvelous and wonderful to behold and enjoy.

It brings:

Liberation from ignorance—the motivation under the gospel of Jesus Christ to develop one's mind. "The glory of God is intelligence, or in other words light and truth." "A man cannot be saved in ignorance." "Whatever principle of intelligence we attain unto in this life, it will rise with us in the resurrection." I should like to say to every one of our sisters that as members of The Church of Jesus Christ of Latter-day Saints you have an obligation to refine and improve your minds and skills, for each of you is a daughter of God with a divine birthright and with an obligation to grow in stature.

Liberation from aimless living—that nonsensical, frilly, fruitless kind of living that so many women engage in. I like the statement of President Stephen L Richards: "Life is a mission and not a career." The Church of Jesus Christ of Latter-day Saints ought to give great purpose to your life.

Liberation from marital insecurity—a partnership under the plan of God with a man you can trust, with a man you can respect, with a man you can honor, with a man you can look to, with a man you can count on, with a man you can help and assist and develop, a companion for time and all eternity who will look to you, in the light of the gospel which he loves and treasures, with respect and honor and dignity and love.

Liberation from loneliness—the company of great and good women of your kind, working together and learning together and growing together and supporting one another. Said Paul to the Romans, "We then that are strong ought to bear the infirmities of the weak," and then he added, "and not to please ourselves." (Romans 15:1.) We have an obligation to develop and grow with one another and support one another, never in the spirit of gossip, always in the spirit of strengthening.

Said the Lord to Peter, ". . . I have prayed for thee, that thy faith fail not: and when thou art converted, strengthen thy brethren." (Luke 22:32.)

To the sisters of the Church I should like to say: When thou art converted, strengthen one another.

Liberation from inferiority. You are not serfs. You are not chattels. You are not dolls. You are daughters of God, queens with a divine birthright and a marvelous eternal future. Lift your heads and smile and walk in the dignity of your birthright.

God bless you so to do!

This challenging question was
given at a devotional assembly
at Brigham Young University

8

Believe in What?

While waiting for a plane in Kansas City, I picked up a copy of a magazine that featured a sixty-four-page supplement on "College Life in America." Written by some very able people who have made some careful analyses, it is a provocative series. It paints a rather dismal picture. It portrays our educational process as a dreary assemblage of "detailed and often absurd course requirements," in which "the college program becomes an obstacle rather than an opportunity," and the student's relationship with his professor is confined merely to "figuring out what he wants and giving it to him."

It deals with the serious problem of sex in our universities. It speaks at length on what is described as "the wasted classroom." It treats the noisy stuff of student politics, the "pedantry and rebellion" of student magazines, and, significantly, the deplorable failure of faculties to bring God into the curriculum.

Now it is trite to say that we live in a world dominated by computers, equations, statistics, charts, surveys, polls, time-and-motion studies. Our students go to college to develop skills in the manipulation of these scientific tools so that the world may recognize them and compensate them. But they must never forget that behind all of these sciences still stands man, a

47

fragile creature in the universe, a creature of emotions, and loneliness, and yearnings. The heart, as well as the hand and the mind, needs educating.

With that premise before me, I turn to a theme from the scriptures. Following the resurrection, the Lord appeared to his apostles. Thomas was not present, and he said that he would not believe unless he saw with his own eyes and felt with his own hands. Eight days later the resurrected Lord appeared again and Thomas was present. And the Lord said, "Reach hither thy finger, and behold my hands; and reach hither thy hand, and thrust it into my side: and *be not faithless, but believing.*" (John 20:27. Italics added.)

That is what I wish to say to our youth: "Be not faithless, but believing." I am prompted to say this because of the cynicism of these articles to which I have referred.

In what shall you believe?

Believe in yourself. The Primary children of the Church sing a great hymn. It stirs me every time I hear it: "I am a child of God."

I recently talked with a young man, an able young man, who had tried to take his life—a young man of promise, of ability, but who was defeated, as everyone feels defeated on occasion. The only remedy he saw was to do away with himself.

Most of the work of the world is done by ordinary people. There are thousands of men with high I.Q.'s who contribute little or nothing to the world, while there are tens of thousands of people of ordinary good sense who run great institutions and fill great responsibilities.

I do not disparage scholarship. I do not uphold mediocrity—I believe in excellence. But each one of us has a place. Each is a child of God. Each of us has great capacity. There is not a man or woman among us who lives up to his or her potential. Each of us has greater capacity than we are now using.

Believe in yourself and be not faithless, but go forward to make the most of what you have, and do not let anybody destroy your determination.

I was inspired while talking with a young missionary serving in the Orient. He was having a rough time. He was not a great scholar. The language appeared impossible to him. But he got on his knees and pleaded with the Lord. He looked me in the eye and said, "I'll do it. I'll make it." He has made it. He has become the means of baptizing people into the Church since I talked with him, and how sweet is his joy.

On the same occasion that I talked with him, I talked with another young man of great capacity and excellent scholarship who has failed because he refused to humble himself and get down and plead with the Lord for that strength which, added to his natural capacity, would have made of him a giant.

Each of us is a child of God. The Lord has planted within our heads and within our hearts the capacity to do worthwhile things. There is not one single soul who cannot do good and worthwhile things.

One young man in one of the missions was sent home sick. He said to me, "My mission is a failure."

I said, "How do you know?"

He said, "I have come home sick."

I said, "Let's get you on your feet. Maybe you can try again."

He went to the doctor, and the doctor treated him for three months. He was a dismal prospect. But he pleaded to go back into the mission field. He spent thirteen months wrapping books because he could not stand the rigors of regular missionary work.

I was there when he finally left to go home. We tallied up his achievements. While working in the office and teaching the gospel in the evening he had brought into the Church in thirteen months thirty-two converts.

"Be not faithless, but believing." Believe in yourselves, in the spirit which God has planted within you as his child.

Believe in work. It is work that will make the difference in your life. I have been amused and intrigued and somewhat shocked with the program that has been set in motion by some labor leaders to establish a twenty-hour work week. In recent years I have had an assignment in the Orient. I love the Oriental people. I have never been to Communist China, but I have been at the gate of Communist China. I know that there are about 650 million people there. They are receiving education; they are industrious; they are workers. Potentially they are as capable as any people on earth. Their ability to learn is as great. How can our nation hope to compete in the world with twenty hours a week of work?

God ordained that we should work. It is application and it is industry that will spell our future. "Be not faithless, but believing" in the divine right to work, and the divinely given responsibility to apply ourselves to the tasks that stand before us.

We are experiencing a great achievement in missionary endeavor. How is it coming about? It is coming about because the Spirit of the Lord is being poured out upon people. This is the chief reason. But there is another factor. Missionaries are working harder than they have worked before. We have conducted some interesting surveys that indicate that when missionaries work twice the average, they get three and four times the results. And when they work half the average, their accomplishment is zero. Work is the law of growth.

Believe in virtue. One of the most discouraging trends in America today is the immorality found among college students. There is no substitute for virtue. The Lord has placed fornication and adultery second only to murder in the category of sins.

Whenever virtue leaves, sorrow enters, and the sorrow which comes under those circumstances never seems to disappear. I talked with a respected grandmother the other day. She feels bereft and heartbroken. She still carries in her conscience guilt over something that happened when she was nineteen years of age. Oh, how she has worked to try to atone for that which she did foolishly and impetuously. All these years she has lived honorably and rendered outstanding service. But somehow there still burns in her heart a great wound that refuses to heal.

My young friends, "Be not faithless, but believing" —in virtue, in goodness, in decency, in purity, in that which the Lord has declared he would have for his children, *virtue*. It is old-fashioned. It may appear out-of-date. It does not square up with a lot of thinking and teaching, but it is *true*. It is as true as the sunrise in the morning, and its fruits are wonderful and rich and sweet to taste.

I heard a great historian, in my undergraduate days many years ago, say that one of the problems facing young people is that marriage in our society must be postponed from the natural age to the financial age. It is a fact. It requires self-discipline. There is too much tendency to give in.

There is nothing lovelier, there is nothing sweeter, there is nothing finer, there is nothing more ennobling, there is nothing more beautiful in all the world than virtue in young men and women. God has designed that it should be so. "Be not faithless, but believing." And in the light of that belief, and in the light of that faith, practice discipline.

Believe in human dignity. Believe in democracy. Believe in liberty. There is a gnawing skepticism that

51

seems to be spreading over the land. Our responsibility is to keep our homeland strong and to keep it righteous and to keep it free, so that the kingdom of God may spread to all the lands of the earth and bring freedom and light and knowledge and understanding to peoples everywhere, for the ushering in of that era when the Prince of Peace shall come as King of kings and Lord of lords. Do not lose faith in the great ideals of freedom and liberty and democracy. "Be not faithless, but believing," and in the light of that belief and in the strength of that faith go out to make these things secure.

And finally, *believe in God.* Believe that he is a rewarder of them that serve him in righteousness. Believe in God as a person, the Father of our spirits to whom we may go in prayer. There appears to be a growing cynicism among young people today. Oh, it is true that they go to church and worship in increasing numbers. But the vital faith that comes of a knowledge in a personal God to whom we can speak and from whom we can receive strength is the thing that will give us power and capacity and stability to stand up and take our places among the peoples of the earth. This is the faith—the only faith—that will bring peace to this troubled world.

Believe in the Lord Jesus Christ, the Only Begotten in the flesh, the Savior and the Redeemer of the world, "for there is none other name under heaven given among men, whereby we must be saved." (Acts 4:12.) Out of that belief will come a sense of brotherhood and a sense of dignity and a sense of kinship among the peoples of the earth. There will come a realization of that divinity which burns within each of us that will give strength to our characters and fiber to our lives and cause us to walk in decency and kindness and appreciation. We then shall be the kind of men and women who will reflect honor to the Church of which we are members.

I testify that we are truly sons and daughters of God, and that there is within each of us a divine spark which may be kindled and burn not only for the blessing of all with whom we associate as we go forth through our lives, but also for our own blessing and peace and satisfaction and enlightenment.

There is today a growing shift
in the direction of vocational education.
Herein are challenges given at
graduation exercises of the
LDS Business College
in Salt Lake City

9

What Will You Take With You?

It is a delight to be with you. I have spoken at a number of commencements, but I feel a particular pleasure in being with you. In one sense I am a product of the LDS Business College. My father and mother met at this institution. My father was head of the business department at Brigham Young University in Provo. This Church school in Salt Lake City was in trouble, and my father was asked by leaders of the Church to come to Salt Lake City and direct this institution. My mother was the first Gregg shorthand teacher in the state of Utah. She taught shorthand and English here. They were married in 1909, and I came along a year later.

I was also a student here—for two weeks. When I completed high school in 1928 I had two weeks with nothing to do. I registered for a typing class. We practiced for those two weeks on a card on which was imprinted the keyboard. I never became an expert typist, but I did learn the keyboard. And these fingers, using that meager knowledge, briefly taught, have since hammered out many hundreds of thousands of words that have become books, pamphlets, radio and television scripts, talks, and other writings. I am grateful for those two weeks. I count them as among the most fruitful and beneficial schooling I ever received. I never took another typing lesson, but the little that I had has proved of inestimable value. When writing I can do it with much greater facility through my fingers at my old manual typewriter than in any other way.

But enough of that. I am not here to talk of myself. I am here to speak to you and of you.

I first want to congratulate you. Your achievements are not trivial. Compare your skills the day you timidly enrolled at this school with this night when you leave with pride.

I commend you for your ambition to learn to do. A substantial part of our social problems today results from a lack of education, which in too many cases results from a lack of ambition. Governments are now spending millions of dollars to train those who lack training, and one of the most difficult problems has been to motivate people to accept this training.

You have come to school through your own desire to improve yourselves. You have paid, as far as possible, your own way. Many of you have worked long hours at various vocations to improve your abilities. You have not asked for favors or special treatment. You have come to equip yourselves to be worth more to your fellowmen.

Now I ask you: *What will you take with you?* I should like to suggest that you take three things and to comment briefly on each:

1. The skill to succeed,
2. The integrity to be trusted,
3. A faith to live by.

The skill to succeed: You have trained yourselves in the nuts and bolts that make our modern economy

55

possible. For one thing, you have been taught to use the English language. What a boon that is—to be able to put words together in such fashion as to cause people to agree with you, to understand you, and to cause them to do things you wish them to do.

You have learned to handle typewriters and other office machines. Without them, our great, pulsing commerce would soon grind to a halt. Any honest executive will tell you that a good secretary will double his capacity. You have learned to make computers talk, and this is fast becoming the language of the world's business.

The introduction of the computer has brought a revolution in our society. You are part of a new age introduced as significantly as was the industrial revolution. Without these marvelous tools there would be no space programs, no supersonic travel, not even the jet airplane or the new high-speed trains. Our banks could not function as they do; our industries would slow to a walk.

What a marvelous thing it is to be a part of this great new revolution, which is improving our standard of living so remarkably. You are the kind who make these things possible. You did not invent the computer. You may not understand the principles on which it operates. But computers are useful only as such people as you learn to use them.

You have developed the skills to succeed. I recently read some of the wisdom of a Chinese philosopher written twenty-six centuries ago. Said Kuan-Tzu: "If you give a man a fish, he will have a single meal. If you teach him how to fish, he will eat all his life."

I once talked with a distinguished judge in Asia. We discussed the problems of his country. He said, "We have too much education." I was shocked at his statement until I found out what he meant. His was one of the emerging nations, a nation that needed people who could do things with their hands, who could handle lathes and drill presses, who could handle typewriters and calculating machines. But instead, the schools were filled with students studying philosophy, history, and sociology. I do not disparage these studies, but I knew what the judge meant when I saw men with doctor's degrees driving taxis and even carrying freight on A-frames on their backs.

You have learned to catch the right kind of fish, and you will eat all your lives. I congratulate you.

The integrity to be trusted: I was not surprised but I was dismayed to read recently of dishonest repairmen who charge high prices for work never done. I hope you have learned in your schooling the meaning of integrity.

Charles Brower, president of a large advertising firm, said some years ago:

This is the great era of the goof-off, the age of the half-done job. The land from coast to coast has been enjoying a stampede away from responsibility. It is populated with laundry men who won't iron shirts, with waiters who won't serve, with carpenters who will come around someday maybe, with executives whose mind is on the golf course, with teachers who demand a single salary schedule so that achievement cannot be rewarded, nor poor work punished, with students who take cinch courses because the hard ones make them think, with spiritual delinquents of all kinds who have been triumphantly determined to enjoy what was known until the present crisis as "the new leisure."

I think that our people are becoming sick of this goofing off. The reason I do not know, but I will guess that we are gradually beginning to realize that history is repeating itself. The Russians are doing a wonderful job as the barbarians in our modern historical drama. But we are far outdoing them in our superlative imitation of Rome. We may lack some of Rome's final decadence, but we do have the two-hour lunch, the three-day weekend, and the all-day coffee break. And, if you want to, you can buy for $275 a jewelled pill box, with a musical built-in alarm that reminds you (but not too harshly) that it's time to take your tranquilizer.

Unquestionably we are in a battle for survival. We must get

our people into the battle. But first we must get some battle into our people.

It has been my privilege over the years to work closely with many men who have been regarded by their associates as great men. I think their predominant quality can be summed up in one word: integrity.

I have heard President David O. McKay say that it is a greater thing to be trusted than to be loved. I believe that. I urge you to take with you the integrity that will merit the trust of your fellowmen.

A faith to live by: The institution from which you are graduated [LDS Business College] was established by men who believed in the living God. Most, if not all, of you have been taking courses in religion along with your secular subjects. Continue to learn of God and his ways. This knowledge is not out of style in this technical age. We never needed it more.

No scheme of life is complete without it. Millions today in many parts of the world look for a fulfillment of their dreams in one false scheme or another. But, say two noted historians, Will and Ariel Durrant, "Heaven and utopia are buckets in a well: when one goes down, the other goes up." (*The Lessons of History,* p. 43.)

It is not enough for you to handle the machines and facilities of commerce as you go out into the world. This sick world needs your faith. Let your example, your words, your witness of the living God and the resurrected Lord Jesus Christ stand as a beacon of faith among your associates.

Years ago a great song was popular with male choruses. It declared: "Give me some men who are stout-hearted men, who will fight for the right they adore. Start me with ten who are stout-hearted men, and I'll soon give you ten thousand more."

Walk in faith and your example will become another's strength. Most of you could stand and testify that the Lord has heard your prayers in days past. He will hear them in days future. Call on him in faith, and he will pour out his blessings upon you.

For a period of eight years Elder Hinckley
served as supervisor of the missions of
the Church in Asia, during which time
he visited South Vietnam
periodically. Out of one of those
experiences came this challenge.

10

A Challenge From Vietnam

In 1967, with Elder Marion D. Hanks, I visited in
Vietnam and other areas of Southeast Asia. In that
troubled part of the world we had many inspiring and
sobering experiences as we met with our brethren in
the armed forces—not only American, but also a few
British and Australian.

Particularly sobering were our meetings in South
Vietnam. Our first stop was the great military base at
Da Nang. There in the base chapel we were greeted by
our brethren, most of whom looked so young. Their
automatic rifles were stacked along the rear pews, and
they sat in their battle fatigues, many of them with a
pistol on the right hip and a knife on the left.

They had come down from the Rock Pile, Marble
Mountain, and other hot and deadly places whose
names were only words in our newspapers, but which
to them were battlegrounds where life is ever so fragile
with the smell of death in the air.

We spent an afternoon in Da Nang in religious ser-
vices that included a memorial for three of their num-

ber recently killed in action. Following that we talked with them individually for hours.

It is a sobering experience to converse with a young Marine who grew up in a quiet western country town, a boy who had been sent off to war and who had just come through forty-two days of deadly battle. He had seen sixty-eight of his company of seventy killed. He had been sickened by the atrocities inflicted by the enemy on the helpless native population. He, like most of his associates, was not there of his own wish, but in response to an obligation imposed upon him; and without fanfare or heroics, he was doing his duty honorably as he understood that duty.

I turned to another young man who stood beside him. He was a handsome boy, tall, clean-faced, wholesome in looks. Hoping to relieve the somber tone of my conversation with the first young man, I said lightly and half jokingly, "What are you going to do when you go home? Have you ever thought of it?"

A wistful sort of light came into his eyes. "Have I ever thought of it? I think of little else, sir. We're moving north again tomorrow, and if I can last another two months I know exactly what I'm going to do when I go home. I'm going to do three things. First, I'm going back to school and finish my education so that I can earn a living at something worthwhile.

"I'm also going to work in the Church and try to do some good. I've seen how desperately the world needs what the Church has to offer.

"And then I'm going to find me a beautiful girl and marry her forever."

I countered with a question, "Are you worthy of that kind of a girl?"

"I hope so, sir," he said. "It hasn't been easy to walk through this filth. It's been pretty lonely at times. But you know, I couldn't let my folks down. I know what my mother expects. I know what she's saying in her prayers. She'd rather have me come home dead than unclean."

I didn't sleep well that night. For one thing, it was terribly hot and the bed was not comfortable. For another, every few minutes a Phantom jet would roar overhead. And beyond that was the statement of this young man who was about to go north again to face possible death.

I don't know whether he lived or died. I am sorry that I do not remember his name. We met and talked with so many and our schedule was so heavy that I do not recall his name or where he was from, but I have not forgotten him. I thought of him when I returned and read of the growing multitude of so-called hippies, of glue-sniffers, goofball addicts, and makers and partakers of other mind-deadening and destroying drugs. I thought of him when I talked with a school dropout who had come to think it more important to buy an old jalopy than to go on with his education. I thought of him when I talked with two young people, the one a once-beautiful girl and the other a once-handsome young man, who had blighted their lives in walking a sordid trail of immorality.

The young Marine mentioned three things he wanted to do and then spoke indirectly of another he was already doing. Out of these I would like to formulate four challenges to youth. They are based on his statement and on the vital gospel in which he and I believe. Though these challenges may sound trite and old-fashioned, I hope you will not close your minds to them. All that is old is not necessarily unworthy, as this young man had concluded while walking the lonely jungle patrols of Vietnam. Nor is all that is new necessarily good, as I have concluded while observing young people throwing their lives away in debilitating practices.

I therefore offer you these challenges:

1. That you prepare for usefulness.
2. That you serve with faith.
3. That you walk in virtue.
4. That you marry for eternity.

Prepare for Usefulness. If ever there was a gospel, it is the gospel of work. Jehovah established the law when he declared, "In the sweat of thy face shalt thou eat bread. . . ." (Genesis 3:19.)

Without labor there is neither wealth, nor comfort, nor progress. It was said of old, ". . . the drunkard and the glutton shall come to poverty: and drowsiness shall clothe a man with rags." (Proverbs 23:21.)

Not long before his death, President John F. Kennedy spoke from the podium in the Salt Lake Tabernacle. At the conclusion of his address, the Tabernacle Choir sang with a majesty it has never excelled, "Mine eyes have seen the glory of the coming of the Lord. . . . His truth is marching on."

As the sound rolled through that historic building, touching the emotions of everyone assembled, I felt a catch in my throat and a tingle in my spine, not alone for the presence there of the chief executive of the United States, not alone for the magnificent music of the choir, but more especially for the quiet men of faith and vision who more than a century ago laid the stone of the great buttresses that formed the walls of that historic Tabernacle and that encircled us and supported the roof that sheltered us. They were people possessed of a dream of destiny. Notwithstanding the fact that they were largely isolated in a desert land, notwithstanding the fact that they erected this building before ever the railroad came to that part of the country, they built with an excellence unsurpassed in our time. They possessed the skill, they nurtured the dream, and they labored with devotion to make that magnificent structure a reality.

Today one need not look far to witness a growing tendency toward superficiality and irresponsibility. I hope that all people, and particularly youth, will see in the Salt Lake Tabernacle an example of the fruits of excellence. I do not expect that all shall pursue academic training. But I would hope that all would seek to develop skills and abilities with which to make a contribution to the world in which they live.

For the more than a century that the Tabernacle has been an assembly place for our people, there has gone forth from that pulpit the counsel of wise and inspired men to each new generation to secure that preparation which will make them useful to society, bring satisfaction to their lives, assure their families the comforts and graces that alone come of effort, and dignify their divine inheritance as sons and daughters of God.

Serve with Faith. The world so much needs young men and women who love the Lord and who will work to build his kingdom.

Soon after my visit to Vietnam, I received a phone call from an officer who had just returned from there. I had met him when we were there and had heard him speak of his reluctance to go to Asia. It was not easy to leave his wife and seven children, including triplet sons three years of age. "But," he said, "I resolved I would give the Air Force the best I had, and I would try to help my brethren in the Church."

He went on to say quietly but earnestly, "I think I have done a better work there than I have ever done before in my life."

I can bear witness to the great good he did. Not only was he highly honored by his government and the government of South Vietnam, but his good example and his faithful service under difficult circumstances also brought religious activity into the lives of hundreds of men.

To young people everywhere I should like to say that you need the Church, and the Church needs you. There is no better association than that with other young men and women of faith who recognize God as their Eternal Father and Jesus Christ as the living Savior of the world. That association will give you strength. It will give you companionship. It will challenge your abilities. It will afford you opportunity for growth. In The Church of Jesus Christ of Latter-day Saints there is office and responsibility for all.

I have seen backward men become giants as they have served in the work of the Lord. The cause of Christ does not need critics; it needs workers. And to restate an old quotation, "Whether you think you can, or whether you think you can't, you're right."

To those of this generation the Lord has said, "... be not weary in well-doing, for ye are laying the foundation of a great work. And out of small things proceedeth that which is great. Behold, the Lord requireth the heart and a willing mind. . . ." (D&C 64:33-34.)

That, my young friends, is the substance of the matter: "the Lord requireth the heart and a willing mind."

Walk in Virtue. To illustrate this great challenge, may I refer to some stirring and inspirational words of President David O. McKay:

In this day when modesty is thrust into the background, and chastity is considered an outmoded virtue, I appeal to parents especially, and to my fellow teachers, both in and out of the Church, to teach youth to keep their souls unmarred and unsullied from this and other debasing sins, the consequences of which will smite and haunt them intimately until their conscience is seared and their character becomes sordid. A chaste, not a profligate, life is the source of virile manhood. The test of true womanhood comes when the woman stands innocent at the court of chastity. All qualities are crowned by this most precious virtue of beautiful womanhood. It is the most vital part of the foundation of a happy married life, and is the source of strength and perpetuity of the race. (*Conference Report,* April 1967.)

To this I wish to add a divine promise uttered long ago by the Savior of the world: "Blessed are the pure in heart: for they shall see God." (Matthew 5:8.)

Marry for Eternity. My young friend in Vietnam was not simply indulging a romantic dream when he said he planned to return and find a beautiful girl and marry her forever. One of the distinguishing features of The Church of Jesus Christ of Latter-day Saints is a belief in the divine nature of the family as an institution ordained of God. Here center the most sacred of all human relationships. Life is eternal. Love is eternal. And God our Eternal Father designed and has made it possible that our families shall be eternal.

In that great colloquy between the apostles and the Christ wherein the Savior asked, "Whom say ye that I am?" and Peter answered, "Thou art the Christ, the Son of the living God," Jesus went on to say, "And I will give unto thee the keys of the kingdom of heaven: and whatsoever thou shalt bind on earth shall be bound in heaven. . . ." (See Matthew 16:5-19.)

That same priesthood authority has been restored to earth by the same Peter, James, and John who received it anciently and it is exercised today in the temples of the Church. Those who kneel at the altars in these holy houses are not joined only until death. They are sealed for all eternity as families.

Not too long after my trip to Vietnam, I was with a wonderful couple who had come all the way from Korea to enter the Salt Lake Temple, there to be joined together for time and for eternity under the authority of the Holy Priesthood. Their faith, like the faith of that young Marine in Southeast Asia, was such that no sacrifice was too great, no cost too high to bind together forever those whom they love most.

I give you my witness and my testimony that this authority is among us today, and I invoke upon you, my choice young friends, the blessings of heaven as you go forward with your lives, that you may choose those values which are enduring.

*To the BYU student body of 25,000
was given a charge to get ready
for the challenges of the future*

11

Prepare to Lead

A few years ago I was in the office of the ambassador to the United States from Argentina. We had been having some difficulty in that country with reference to visas for our missionaries, and in an effort to resolve that problem, we called on the ambassador.

We told him that we had about 300 missionaries in Argentina, all of whose cases were under appeal, which we regarded as a very serious situation. Then we set forth our testimony and arguments. The president of the Argentina North Mission, who had come up for this purpose, brought out some photographs of his missionaries and said, "Mr. Ambassador, these are the young men and women we are talking about." They were a handsome lot—clean-cut, well-groomed, smart-looking young men and women.

The ambassador made a complimentary remark. Then I ventured to say something like this:

"Thirty-five years ago I served as a missionary in England. As long as I live I will never lose my love for that great and interesting and fascinating part of the world. I was not there as a tourist. I was in the homes of the people and came to know their hearts, and no one can ever sell the British short with me.

"Now," I said, "here are 300 young men and women in your land. They have had a year or two of university work and they will come back and enter school again. They will go on to become doctors and lawyers and politicians, leaders of business and government, teachers, scientists, and artists. But as long as they live they will never lose their love for Argentina. They are working there with the people. They know the beauty and the temper of your land. They know the hearts of your people. They will return home and marry, and it will be one of the dreams of their lives to take their sweethearts back to the land in which they labored as missionaries."

I said, "I'm not so concerned about today as I am about twenty years from today, as I look ahead and envision these young men and women, when they shall be filling positions of leadership. I want them to carry with them always an appreciation for your land and your people."

I am satisfied that those young men and women, if they keep the faith, will become leaders. The assurance of this was impressed more firmly on my mind recently when I met, as I have opportunity once in a while, with a group of men who were together as missionaries in England nearly forty years ago.

In 1935, at the conclusion of a great conference, about fifteen of us gathered together in a hotel room in Kidderminster, England, and resolved we would try to keep the spirit of the wonderful association we had there while serving the Lord.

Two of these men have passed away. At the time of his death, one was a vice-president of the Columbia Broadcasting System and a member of the general superintendency of the Young Men's Mutual Improvement Association. Among those who still meet together are three university professors, one university department head, four business executives of prominence, three lawyers, one doctor, and a university president.

As for their church activities, there are two bishops and a counselor in a bishopric, a high councilor, a member of a stake presidency, four members of general boards, three Regional Representatives of the Twelve, and a member of the Council of the Twelve. Four decades ago they were ordinary young men serving as missionaries for the Church.

The great purpose of our institutions of higher learning, as I see it, is not only to impart secular knowledge and spiritual strength, but to develop leaders.

In my visits to South America, the Orient, and other parts of the world, I have seen millions upon millions of people living in poverty, struggling to keep alive; and I have said to myself, again and again, this is our opportunity and this is our challenge and this is our obligation: to teach them and train them and light within their hearts the spark and fire of leadership among their people. Oh, how great is the need and how tremendous is the opportunity! To every young man and young woman in the Church I give this challenge: *Prepare to lead!*

General Mark Clark is reported to have said:

All nations seek it constantly because it is the key to greatness, sometimes to survival—the electric and elusive quality known as leadership. Where does juvenile delinquency begin? In leaderless families. Where do slums fester? In leaderless cities. Which armies falter? Which political parties fail? Leaderless ones. Contrary to the old saying that leaders are born and not made, the art of leading can be taught and it can be mastered.

In an article titled "How the Effective Executive Does It," Peter Drucker, Jr., made this interesting conclusion, which was a great comfort to me and ought to be to some of you: "Executive ability seems to have little correlation with intelligence, imagination, or brilliance." Then he goes on to say that the good executive (1) practices conservation of time, (2) has his eye fixed on new developments, (3) builds on the strengths of his colleagues, and (4) starves the problems and feeds the opportunities.

It has been my opportunity over the years to work with great men; I think this has been the most fruitful blessing of my life. And I also have concluded that you do not have to have a tremendous I.Q. to be a leader, to be successful. Most of the work of the world is not done by geniuses. It is done by ordinary people who have learned to apply what talents and capacities they have to the responsibilities that they have accepted. The Lord said something significant when he stated these great words:

> . . . seek ye diligently and teach one another words of wisdom; yea, seek ye out of the best books words of wisdom; seek learning, *even by study and also by faith.* (D&C 88:118. Italics added.)

The greatest opportunity for you, our youth, is to qualify yourselves in the skills of which you dream. Don't muff it. Don't drift. Take advantage of the opportunities to improve your skills in your chosen fields. Seek learning by study, and seek it also by faith, and "God shall give unto you knowledge by his Holy Spirit, yea, by the unspeakable gift of the Holy Ghost. . . ." (D&C 121:26.)

Oh, how we need in this day and time men and women who will stand up for decency and truth and honesty and virtue and law and order and all of the other good qualities on which our society is founded. *Get involved.* Get involved on the side of righteousness. You, and others like you, are the great hope of this world. I love these words of Paul to Agrippa when he recounted his experience on the way to Damascus. The Lord spoke to him and said, when he had fallen to the ground:

71

But rise, and stand upon thy feet: for I have appeared unto thee for this purpose, to make thee a minister and a witness. . . . To open their eyes, and to turn them from darkness to light, and from the power of Satan unto God. . . . (Acts 26:16, 18.)

The problem with most of us is that we are afraid. We want to do the right thing, but we are troubled by fears and we sit back and the world drifts about us.

I confess to you that by nature I was a very timid boy. When I left to go on a mission my good father said, "I want to give you only one verse of scripture." I think this has become perhaps the greatest help of my life. They are the words of the Lord to the ruler of the synagogue whose daughter was reported dead, and the Lord turned to the ruler and said, "Be not afraid, only believe." (Mark 5:36.)

I commend to you these wonderful words of the Lord as you think of your responsibilities and opportunities.

The Church of Jesus Christ of Latter-day Saints is not a little tucked-away organization. It is the kingdom of God in the earth. This is the stone which was cut out of the mountain without hands, which should roll forth and fill the whole earth. This is the cause of which the prophets dreamed and spoke. This is the kingdom of the Lord Jesus Christ restored in this the greatest dispensation of all time, to bless the people of the earth with the truth, the living truth of the living God. How we need men and women of strength and stature and faith and persuasiveness who will stand as advocates of the truth of God. And the marvelous thing is, you can do it!

Do not be afraid to accept responsibility in the kingdom. The Lord will never ask you to do anything that you cannot do.

I gain comfort from Moses. The Lord called him to lead Israel out of Egypt. This herder of sheep, this fugitive, was to become the savior of Israel. And Moses pleaded his weakness and said:

O my Lord, I am not eloquent, . . . but I am slow of speech, and of a slow tongue.

And the Lord said unto him, Who hath made man's mouth? . . .

Now therefore go, and I will be with thy mouth, and teach thee what thou shalt say. (Exodus 4:10-12.)

God bless you with the faith to go forward, trusting that the Lord will be with you and teach you what you shall say as you stand in positions of leadership in building the kingdom of God in the earth.

I go back to these great words of General Clark: "Where does juvenile delinquency begin? In leaderless families."

I sat for three hours one evening listening to two young men, one at a time, young men with difficult and serious problems, young men who had been called to positions of great trust and who came to say they could not accept because they were unworthy. Each unraveled a tale, disheartening and troubled and tragic, as he sat weeping across the desk. I found that one came from a home where there was drunkenness and bitterness and tension and strife. And the other came from a home where there was separation and divorce and meanness and vindictiveness; and I thought of the words spoken long ago: ". . . whatsoever a man soweth, that shall he also reap." (Galatians 6:7.)

It has been my responsibility over the years to talk with hundreds of young men and women who have had serious troubles, and I have found that in nearly every case each has come out of a troubled home.

I want to say to all our youth: You cannot afford to be anything less than the best insofar as your family relationships are concerned. The fruits are too important. The consequences are too eternal to take a chance on anything less than the right thing. God bless you to go forward with faith to do what the Lord would have you do, living with respect one for another, and affection and love and concern.

When all is said and done, love isn't a matter of romance; it is an anxious concern for the well-being and the comfort of one's companion. How much happier the world would be if there were a greater measure of happiness in the homes of the people! If there were mothers who walked in dignity and virtue and truth and kindness, and fathers who stood at the heads of their homes as men of virtue and goodness and faith and faithfulness!

God bless you, my dear young brethren and sisters, as youth of the noble birthright, to prepare to lead. The world needs you. It will make a place for you, and you will fill it as you should if you walk in light and truth according to the principles of the gospel of Jesus Christ.

In August 1973 Latter-day Saints gathered
from seven nations of Europe in a great
conference held in the Olympic Sports
Hall in Munich, Germany. Most were converts
who have known something of the meaning
of loneliness

12

The Loneliness of Leadership

I have seen many beautiful sights in Europe—the towering Alps that rise from the valleys of Germany, Switzerland, Austria, France, and Italy; the great rivers that flow to the sea from the melting snows of these magnificent mountains; crystal lakes that lace the landscape; forests that are dark with their own foreboding beauty; the quaint villages; the well-kept farms; the galleries of art; the architecture that speaks of great skill and enduring design.

I have looked at these with wonder and respect, and even reverence; but I think I have never seen a more beautiful picture, a more inspiring sight, than this congregation of Latter-day Saints gathered from many of the nations of Europe. Your faces radiate the spirit of the gospel. In your presence one feels the strength of personal testimony. There are thousands of you here today. You feel the warmth of one another's faith, the strength of one another's companionship.

But it was not always so. Most of you are converts to the Church who passed through the difficult struggle of conversion. You have known loneliness and heartache. You have fasted and prayed and pleaded, recognizing first a glimmer of truth, and then fighting to gain that knowledge which made all else seem relatively unimportant.

Today in this conference, you feel part of a great pulsating organization. In this association together there is peace and security. When you leave to return to your homes, to your employment, to the small branches from which many of you come, to the association of those who do not see as you see and do not think as you think, and who are prone to ridicule, you may feel again that loneliness.

But as members of the Church, you have become as a city set upon a hill whose light cannot be hid. To those about you, you are different, just as the true gospel is different from the philosophies of the world. And whether you like it or not, each of you is set apart. You are partakers of the truth, and with that comes a responsibility. Testimony is a personal thing, and its responsibilities are personal.

It was Queen Victoria who said, "Uneasy rests the head that wears the crown." This has been the history of those serving in the cause of Christ.

When in this dispensation the Lord declared this to be "the only true and living church upon the face of the whole earth" (D&C 1:30), we were immediately put in a position of loneliness, the loneliness of leadership from which we cannot shrink nor run away, and which we must face up to with boldness and courage and without compromise. Every true convert has passed through it. Every true member of this Church who lives and breathes the spirit of the gospel as he associates with others knows something of that feeling. But once having gained a testimony, a man has to live with it. A man has to live with his conscience. A man has to live with God.

It was ever thus. The price of leadership is loneliness. The price of adherence to conscience is loneliness. The price of adherence to principle is loneliness.

I think it is inescapable. The Savior of the world was one who walked alone much of the time. I know of no statement more underlined with the pathos of loneliness than his statement: "The foxes have holes, and the birds of the air have nests; but the Son of Man hath not where to lay his head." (Matthew 8:20.) There is no lonelier picture in all history than that of Jesus upon the cross, alone, the Redeemer of mankind, the Savior of the world, bringing to pass the atonement, the Son of God suffering for the sins of mankind.

Not long ago we stood with President Harold B. Lee in the Garden of Gethsemane in Jerusalem. We could sense, if only in a very small degree, the terrible struggle that took place there, a struggle so intense as Jesus wrestled alone in the spirit that blood came from every pore.

In imagination we saw again the betrayal by one who had been called to a position of great trust. We saw evil men lay brutal hands upon the Son of God. And then into our minds came the picture of that lonely figure on the cross, crying out in anguish, "My God, my God, why hast thou forsaken me?" (Matthew 27:46.)

When the tyranny of religious oppression was smothering Europe, there arose a man here and there who stood up in quiet defiance. I believe that the Reformers were inspired of God to lay the foundation for a time when another angel would fly through "the midst of heaven, having the everlasting gospel to preach unto them that dwell on the earth, and to every nation, and kindred, and tongue, and people." (Revelation 14:6.) It was in Germany where with courage, but in loneliness, Martin Luther proclaimed his ninety-five theses. That which he and his associates and followers endured is a matter of history. As they led the way to a more enlightened age, they walked almost alone amid the scoffing of the crowd.

The Prophet of this dispensation was a man of

loneliness. The fourteen-year-old boy who came out of the woods was hated and persecuted. Can you sense something of his loneliness as reflected in these words:

". . . while they were persecuting me, reviling me, and speaking all manner of evil against me falsely . . . , I was led to say in my heart: Why persecute me for telling the truth? I have actually seen a vision; and who am I that I can withstand God, or why does the world think to make me deny what I have actually seen? For I had seen a vision; I knew it, and I knew that God knew it, and I could not deny it. . . ." (Joseph Smith 2:25.)

There are few more sorrowful pictures than of the Prophet Joseph being rowed across the Mississippi River knowing that his enemies were after his life. And then there even came some of his own who accused him of running away. Under those circumstances he said, "If my life is of no value to my friends, it is of none to myself." (*Documentary History of the Church* 6:549.)

He returned and was taken to Carthage where on June 27, 1844, he was killed, a martyr to the truth.

His successors have likewise known much loneliness in the great and sacred trust they have filled as Presidents of the Church. But not they alone. Many of you have known the desolation that comes to a convert as he leaves old associations to enter the waters of baptism and begin a new course of life.

I have been thinking of a friend whom I knew when I was on a mission in London forty years ago. He came to our apartment through the rain of the night. He knocked at the door, and I invited him in.

He said, "I have to talk to someone. I'm all alone."
I asked, "What is your problem?"
He said, "When I joined the Church my father told

me to get out of his house and never come back. A few
months later my athletic club dropped me from mem-
bership. Last month my boss fired me because I'm a
member of this church. And last night the girl I love
said she would never marry me because I'm a Mormon."

I said, "If this has cost you so much, why don't you
leave the Church and go back to your father's home,
and to your club, and to the job that meant so much to
you, and to the girl you think you love?"

He said nothing for what seemed a long time. Then,
putting his head in his hands, he sobbed as if his heart
would break. Finally he looked up through his tears
and said, "I couldn't do that. I know this is true, and
if it were to cost me my life I could never give it up."
He picked up his wet hat and walked to the door and
out into the rain, alone and trembling and fearful, but
resolute. As I watched him, I thought of the loneliness
of conscience, the loneliness of faith, and of the
strength and power of personal testimony.

To you who are here today, and particularly you
young men and women, I should like to say that you
may come to know much of loneliness as members of
The Church of Jesus Christ of Latter-day Saints. In the
days and the months and the years to follow, you may
find yourselves very much in the minority in the world
in which you walk. You will feel the loneliness of your
faith.

It is not easy, for instance, to be virtuous when all
about you there are those who scoff at virtue.

It is not easy to be temperate when all about you
there are those who scoff at sobriety.

It is not easy to be a man or woman of integrity
when about you there are those who forsake principle
for expediency.

It is not easy to speak in testimony of the divinity

of the Lord Jesus Christ to those who would mock him and belittle and demean him.

I should like to say that there is much of loneliness, but a man of your kind has to live with his conscience. A man has to live with his principles, a man has to live with his convictions. A man has to live with his testimony. Unless he does so, he will be miserable, dreadfully miserable. And while there may be thorns, while there may be disappointments, while there may be trouble and travail, heartache and heartbreak and desperate loneliness, there will be peace and comfort and strength.

I think Paul wrote of your kind when he said to Timothy, "God hath not given us the spirit of fear; but of power, and of love, and of a sound mind. Be not thou therefore ashamed of the testimony of our Lord. . . ." (2 Timothy 1:7-8.)

To those who are not ashamed, and to those who will speak forth with courage, the Lord has declared: ". . . I will go before your face. I will be on your right hand and on your left, and my Spirit shall be in your hearts, and mine angels round about you, to bear you up." (D&C 84:88.)

This is a promise. I believe it; I know it; I bear testimony of its truth to you this day. God bless you, you of the covenant, you young men and women who are the greatest hope of this generation, you noble youth of great ability and tremendous potential.

God bless you to walk fearlessly even though you walk alone, and to know in your hearts that peace which comes of squaring one's life with principle, that "peace which passeth all understanding."

INDEX

McKay, David O., how to gain
  wisdom, 36-37; trust is greater than
  love, 58; value of chastity, 65.
Meekness, meek to inherit the earth,
  13.
Mind, enrichment and discipline of,
  38, 45.
Missionary program, 19, 25.
Missionary work, 49, 50, 64, 68-69.
Morality, not out-moded by modern
  tradition, 30.
Mormon, foreordained as a leader, 16.
Moses, example of strength and
  performance of duty, 72-73.
Murder, most grievous of sins, 51.

-N-
Nephi, foreordained by God, 16.
New Guinea, 22.
"New Morality," attitudes of sexual
  impurity detrimental to freedom,
  1-6; on campus, 30.

-O-
Obedience, essential to salvation
  and freedom, 19, 21.

-P-
Paul, 46, 80.
Peace, inner, gained through purity
  and obedience to God's command-
  ments, 1-8; 18, 19, 21, 24, 31.
Peter, 46.
Pioneers, struggles of in early Church,
  10-11, 63.
Pollock, Channing, purity, 7.
Pornography, reaping whirlwind of
  decay, 5-6; violates the priesthood,
  18; wastes precious time, 37.
Posterity, right to be born into
  purity, 19.
Potential, great through divine
  birthright, 17, 21, 45, 48, 49, 71.
Poverty, 12, 63, 70.
Prayer, to gain strength, 19, 20-21,
  36-37, 49, 52, 59.
Priesthood, authority of restored to the
  earth, 66-67.
Priesthood bearers, responsibility of
  to magnify callings, 20; to be pure,
  18.
Promiscuity, destroys freedom, 5-6;
  on campus, 50-51.

Purity, protects freedom, 6-7; peace
  of mind through, 18-19; importance
  of to women, 43; renders
  worthiness for blessings, 44; no
  substitute for, 51; true test of
  womanhood, 65-66; President
  David O. McKay's teachings
  concerning, 65-66.
Purpose, important in establishing
  goals, 45, 63.

-Q-
Queen Victoria, loneliness of
  leadership, 76.

-R-
Reading, good literature, 37, 42.
Reformers, the, inspired of God, 77.
Relief Society, gain intelligence
  through the, 45.
Repentance, solution to marital
  problems, 26.
Responsibility, as leaders in
  the gospel, 76.
Resurrection, of Christ, 45.
Richards, Stephen L, "Life is a
  mission and not a career," 45.
Ridicule, ways to gain strength
  through, 76.
Rome, decline of, through immorality
  and laziness, 6, 57, 58.
Russell, Bertrand, "The curse of
  America is conformity," 36.

-S-
Sacrifice, essential to true worship
  of God, 23-24; basis of friendship,
  26.
Salt Lake Tabernacle, example of
  industry, 63-64.
Samuel, foreordained by God, 16.
Self-discipline, importance of in
  progression towards perfection,
  5, 21, 30, 38, 39, 51.
Self-respect, 3-4, 31, 48.
Selfishness, basis of trouble, 24-25;
  overcome by service, 26-27; roots
  of evil, 27.
Serve the Lord, 41, 64.
Service, brings blessings to others,
  14, 18, 21, 24; lose self through,
  25, 27, 41, 64, 65.
Shakespeare, William, quoted, 39, 41.

Index

Skill, education develops, 56, 63;
   necessary for success, 71.
Sorrow, follows loss of virtue, 51.
"Sound of Music," The, 17.
Spirit, nourish the, 39-40.
Stone, cut out of the mountain, 72.
Strength, through the fulfillment of
   responsibilities, 19, 21; needed for
   the future, 32; through cleanliness
   and obedience, 38-39, 40, 46, 59, 65,
   66, 72.
Success, developing skills necessary
   for, 56, 71.

-T-
Teach, the responsibility to, 70-71.
Tennyson, Alfred Lord, "My
   strength is the strength of ten,
   Because my heart is pure," 4.
Testimony, of Christ, 32; gives strength
   in troubled times, 76-80.
Thanksgiving, essential to express
   appreciation, 11-14.
Time, wise use of, 36, 70.
Timidity, how to overcome, 72.
Trust, essential in marriage, 45;
   begets integrity, 57-58.
Truth, 36, 45.

-U-
Understanding, how to gain, 29, 52.
Unwed mothers, dilemma of, 4.
Usefulness, importance of, 63.

-V-
Values, importance of adopting good,
   4, 67.
Van Buren, Abigail, advice on sexual
   immorality, 43-44.
Vietnam, lessons of sacrifice and
   courage, 4, 60-67.
Virtue, essential for freedom and
   peace through righteousness, 2-8,
   18, 30-31, 43-44, 50-51, 65-66, 71, 74,
   79.
Virtuous thoughts, essential for
   confidence in the presence of God,
   6-7, 37.

-W-
War, 22; Vietnamese, 60-67.
Weakness, how to overcome, 46.
Wisdom, requires effort, 36.
Women, 42-46; chastity the true mark
   of womanhood, 65-66.
Women's liberation, through the
   gospel, 44-45.
Woodruff, Wilford, 15, 19-20.
Word of Wisdom, strength gained
   through obedience to, 16, 38-39.
Work, importance of, 18, 48; divine
   right of, 50; integrity of, 57;
   contribution to usefulness, 63-65.
Worship, sacrifice essential to, 24-25.

-Y-
Young, Brigham, 34.
Youth, the future of the Church, 15,
   17.